T2-ECT-915

How to Land the Best Jobs in School Administration

Revised Edition

The Self-Help Workbook for Practicing and Aspiring School Administrators

Georgia J. Kosmoski

CORWIN PRESS, INC.
A Sage Publications Company
Thousand Oaks, California

For information:

Corwin Press, Inc.
A Sage Publications Company
2455 Teller Road
Thousand Oaks, California 91320
E-mail: order@corwinpress.com

SAGE Publications Ltd.
6 Bonhill Street
London EC2A 4PU
United Kingdom

SAGE Publications India Pvt. Ltd.
M-32 Market
Greater Kailash I
New Delhi 110 048 India

Printed in the United States of America

Library of Congress Cataloging-in-Publication Data

ISBN 0-8039-6798-5 (cloth: acid-free paper)
ISBN 0-8039-6799-3 (pbk.: acid-free paper)

99 00 01 02 03 10 9 8 7 6 5 4 3 2 1

Corwin Editorial Assistant: Kristen Gibson
Production Editor: Wendy Westgate
Editorial Assistant: Nevair Kabakian
Designer/Typesetter: Danielle Dillahunt

Contents

Foreword

This self-help workbook is written for you, the serious individual who plans to actively seek a position in school administration. To truly benefit from this workbook, you must be willing to work and work hard. Focus, persistence, and commitment are necessary, but the rewards are great. *How to Land the Best Jobs in School Administration* provides you, an active learner, with experiences and knowledge **to find and secure the right job**. Having gone through this process a number of times myself, I only wish that when I needed it this book was there for me. As the old adage reminds us, "Knowledge Is Power." This book is designed to give you the power to succeed. Use it to help you move up, move laterally, or move into your first administrative position.

Acknowledgments

A special thank you to the 12 professional men and women educators who reviewed this workbook and provided valuable input and suggestions. Kudos to Peg Whitaker who used her talent to create the striking sketches that begin each chapter.

Georgia J. Kosmoski

About the Author

Georgia J. Kosmoski is Professor of Educational Administration at Governors State University, located outside Chicago, Illinois, where she is the only female professor in the program that serves 350 educational administration graduate students, 61% of which are women. She has been an educator for over 25 years. After being a classroom teacher, she earned a dual Ph.D. in school administration and curriculum/instruction from Purdue University and became a school administrator. She has served as an assistant principal, principal, and assistant superintendent. Her research interests include school supervision and the issues that concern beginning, women, and aspiring administrators. She is author of *Supervision* (1997), a school administration text.

Introduction

To secure any position in school administration, you will encounter a series of predetermined and required steps and procedures. As an aspirant, you must formally apply for the position, which includes forwarding a letter of intent, a resume, an optional application, and support documentation. Then, you, the candidate, must successfully hurdle one or more interviews. Next, you must negotiate the initial contract that will affect your work and life conditions for the tenure of the employment. Finally, you must secure or "lock in" your position.

This workbook is designed to help you through each step of the process. It teaches you how to write a professional letter of intent and riveting résumé, how to capitalize on your personal and perceived professional strengths, and how to defuse your own weaknesses and those perceived by selection committees. You learn which selection committees will support or oppose you. This workbook teaches you how to communicate with members of the opposite sex and how to recognize and deal with harassment, coaches you on why and how to do your homework about the position and the district prior to the interview, and instructs you about what interview attire is the most accepted. It provides the most often asked interview questions and encourages you to prepare quality responses. You learn techniques and practices in the art of negotiation that will help you secure an enviable contract. Finally, you receive helpful suggestions for keeping your new job.

All information shared in this workbook was derived from actual field surveys and the current accepted literature. The surveys were conducted in urban, suburban, and rural areas, with primary input coming from urban and suburban sectors. All socioeconomic strata and ethnic populations were represented. Over 600 individuals were extensively interviewed. Men and women administrators who recently landed a desired position, selection committee members, established building and central office administrators, individuals that develop interview pools, and other school constituents participated. Their responses form the database used to determine conclusions and a suggested course of action for you. Many of the strategies, concepts, and practices that you *believed* to be true are now supported with data gathered from frontline participants.

Use the workbook exercises, activities, and information sections to chart a course of action tailor-made for you to acquire your school administration position. If you are not ready to follow the process, you really don't want the job. But if you do follow the suggestions offered and perform the exercises outlined in this workbook, you will be well prepared for success.

NOTE: All names of people and places used in the the case problems, cover letter, and sample résumé are fictitious.

1

Acquiring Your Mentor

Acquiring a devoted and quality mentor to advise and work with you during the job-searching period gives you the extra edge necessary to be successful.

Steps for Securing a Mentor While Job Hunting

1. Review the results of the study examining the value of a job-seeking mentor.

2. Read the rationale for acquiring a mentor for this challenging process.

3. Use self-reflection to determine your choice of mentor.

4. Contact the chosen individual and solicit and secure that person's cooperation and participation. Give the person a copy of *My Mentor's Job Description* provided in this section.

5. With your mentor, complete the contract provided. Give each of you a completed copy.

This Is an Essential: Study Results Prove Success

A study was conducted to determine if there was a difference in success ratio between 50 aspiring school administrators who acquired a mentor and 50 who did not secure a mentor. After 18 months, results were as follows.

	Aspirants With Mentor	*Aspirants Without Mentor*
Average number of submitted applications	13	11.5
Average number of interviews	5	3
Positions acquired	8	4

Conclusions

Acquiring a mentor will help you do the following:

- Learn of and apply for more viable positions
- Have more interviews
- Double your chances of acquiring a position

The Mentor

As school administrators, we see ourselves as confident, self-sufficient, and independent. We often find it difficult to ask for help for ourselves and then to accept good advice. However, when seeking the right administrative position it is the time to break the mold, stop being stubborn, and find help. If you are truly committed to seeking a new position, you must agree to accept the help of a mentor. You can think of and refer to this person as mentor, confidant, or coach, but you need to acquire one right from the outset.

A mentor's help and support will be invaluable during the often long and arduous process of job hunting. A mentor will provide you with that extra confidence, focus, and tenacity required to be successful. Your coach will give you the edge necessary to complete the task.

Choose your mentor wisely. Your best friend is not necessarily your best choice. You must find a person who is willing to expend the required time and effort to be effective. Your mentor should possess a number of characteristics. He or she must be a knowledgeable and experienced administrator. Your mentor should be both a pragmatist and a visionary. She or he must be frank and willing to "tell it like it is," be a person you wish to model, and an active listener. Patience, kindness, humor, and fortitude are qualities that make for an effective mentor. Look for a mentor who will be honest with you in a way that you will not be honest with yourself.

What is your role in this relationship? What must you do to make this a worthwhile endeavor? Your role and responsibilities are simple. The formula is share, listen, and take advice. If you choose to follow this course of action, you must be willing to share information and ask for advice. Next, you must be willing to really listen to the advice, suggestions, and criticism given. Finally, you must be willing to accept the help given to you. If you valued this person's opinion enough to solicit their help, then you seriously must exercise the option of accepting.

What might you do if you cannot identify or secure a quality mentor from the outset? Although this possibility is rare, it could happen. In this case, continue actively searching. If you cannot enlist the perfect person for you, aggressively seek out a good coach. Good is surely better than none. In the interim, rely on this workbook for guidance. Although it cannot replace your mentor, it will provide you with much needed support.

After reading the characteristics of a quality mentor and your expected behaviors on the next page, your first outside task is to identify the ideal mentor for you and then recruit that person. If you make this commitment and follow through, you demonstrate that you are serious about acquiring the right position in school administration. Finally, you and your mentor should complete and sign the contract found near the end of this chapter. This will formalize the relationship.

My Mentor's Job Description

My mentor will be as follows:

- An experienced, knowledgeable, and successful school administrator
- Willing to expend on my behalf the necessary time and effort to be effective
- Both a pragmatist and a visionary
- A role model for me
- Open, candid, and honest with me
- An active listener for me
- Patient, kind, tenacious, and lighthearted

MENTOR'S CONTRACT

On this ________ day of ______________________,
(Month and year)

I, _________________________________, agree to serve as a
(Mentor's name)

job-seeking mentor for ___________________________, from this
(Your name)

date forward for a period of __________________________.
(Specify time period)

To the best of my ability, I will try to maintain close contact with you and remain accessible. I will actively listen, encourage, advise, and support you.

Signature: _______________________________ Date: __________
(Mentor's signature)

Witnessed by: ____________________________ Date: __________
(Your signature)

Case Problem: What I Need

After reading this section, you take time for a coffee break, but a nagging question keeps bothering you. You wonder who you should select as your mentor. You realize that this person will be very important to you in the months to come and you don't want to take any chances and choose poorly. After a few minutes, you realize that you need a mentor who can DELIVER. You need a person who can perform all the tasks of a quality mentor. But what are those tasks? What kinds of roles and behaviors must this person be willing to undertake and accomplish well? If you knew what the person had to do to be the **ideal mentor** you could choose more effectively. **Aha!** A list of mentor tasks would be a great help to you when you make your choice. Make a list of tasks you expect from your future mentor. If you want that person to DELIVER, what do you expect that person to do? *Write your answer below.**

*See Appendix A for one suggested response.

Suggested Readings on the Merits of Mentoring

Glickman, C. D. (1990). Preface. In T. M. Bey & C. Thomas Holmes (Eds.), *Mentoring: Developing successful teachers.* Reston, VA: Association of Teacher Educators.

Goodlad, J. (1990). *Teachers for our nation's schools.* San Francisco: Jossey-Bass.

Hall, G. (1992). Induction: The missing link. *Journal of Education, 33*(3), 53-55.

Healy, C., & Welchert, A. (1990). Mentoring relations: A definition to advance research and practice. *Educational Researcher, 19*(9), 17-21.

Huling-Austin, L. (1990). Mentoring is squishy business. In T. Bey & C. Thomas Holmes (Eds.), *Mentoring: Developing successful teachers.* Reston, VA: Association of Teacher Educators.

Kosmoski, G. J. (1997). *Supervision.* Mequon, WI: Stylex.

Kosmoski, G. J., & Pollack, D. R. (1997). *Effects of a mentoring program for beginning school administrators.* Hilton Head, SC: Eastern Educational Research Association.

Merriam, S. (1993). Mentor and proteges. A critical review of the literature. *Adult Education Quarterly, 33*(3), 161-173.

2

The Quality Cover Letter and Riveting Résumé

The résumé and cover letter serve two purposes. These papers introduce you to the district and act as the enticement to meet you. They transmit the first impression of you to your potential employers and document who and what you are. Obviously, both are crucial to securing the desired position. Great care must be taken when developing your cover letter and résumé. This section helps you determine and design professional documents that use both desirable contract content and format.

Steps to Writing a Polished Cover Letter

1. Read the survey data to learn the characteristics of a desirable cover letter.
2. Study the sample letter of intent.
3. Utilize the suggestions provided to develop your practice draft.
4. As you refer to your "generic" first copy, compose a specific letter of intent. Write a letter that matches the job description of the desired position.

The Cover Letter or Letter of Intent

To write a desirable cover letter or letter of intent, you should do the following:

1. **Include these content components:**

   - Your desire and intent to apply
   - Your reason for applying, with emphasis on match between you and the district
   - Your expectations of a forthcoming interview
   - Your acknowledgment of enclosures

2. **Use a traditional letter format, which includes these elements:**

   - Personal heading or letterhead
   - Inside heading addressed to the person identified as the "contact person"
   - Date
   - Greeting
   - Body
   - Closing
   - Signature

3. **Follow the style guidelines recommended in this section.**

4. **Be thorough, yet succinct. Limit your communication to one page.**

For additional clarification, examine the following sample letter of intent. It should serve as a model or guide.

Then, get your feet wet and write your own "generic" letter of intent. You can use it as a starting point for the real thing when you find a desirable positon.

NOTE: Block or traditional format is acceptable.

Loren W. Moore, Ph.D.
Director of Elementary Curriculum
Happy Haven School District
1234 Bush Drive, Clinton, MA 60602
Phone: 509-333-0012 Fax: 509-333-0013

May 15, 1998

Dr. Walter Green
Assistant Superintendent of Personnel
Perfect School Corporation
Overthere, IN 46322

Dear Dr. Green:

Please accept my application for the position of Assistant Superintendent of Curriculum and Instruction for your school district. After reading the job description I am very pleased to see that this position matches my aspirations, educational preparation, qualifications, experiences, and strengths.

When reading my application and resume, you will see that I have a dual Ph.D. in School Administration and Curriculum/Instruction and the required certification. I have been a successful educator for 20 years. I have served as an elementary teacher, high school assistant principal, middle school principal, and now as Director of Elementary Curriculum. I have enjoyed working in both urban and suburban districts with diverse ethnic populations from various socioeconomic levels.

Along with my qualifications, I bring a true desire to expand my challenges, duties, and responsibilities to a pre-K through 12 setting. I am familiar with the positive reputation and vision of your district and feel that I would be most happy working with you.

Enclosed are my resume, application, copies of my licenses, certificates, transcripts, and support materials highlighting my curriculum activities. I am most excited about our possible future together. I am looking forward to meeting and talking with you and the Perfect School Corporation selection committee in the near future.

Sincerely,

Loren W. Moore, Ph.D.
8 Enclosures

Steps to Constructing Your Riveting Résumé

1. Read the survey results to learn the views of those who develop interview pools regarding résumé positives and negatives.

2. Construct your first résumé draft using the conclusions from the survey.

3. Use the two assessment scales, *Examining the Style and Format of My Résumé* and *Guide for Critiquing a Résumé,* found in this section to evaluate and correct your initial efforts.

4. Ask several (at least two) trusted professional colleagues to do the same. You will need to provide them with a copy of your résumé plus copies of the two following score sheets.

5. Use the feedback gathered from Steps 3 and 4 above to edit and polish your résumé.

6. To ensure improvement, repeat Steps 3 and 4 for your polished second draft.

7. Complete the case problem and then check Appendix A to see if you agree.

8. Remember to update your résumé regularly. Every 6 months is desirable.

What the Survey Data Reveal About the Résumé

What Should I Include and Exclude?

Superintendents, assistant superintendents, and other individuals responsible for developing an interview pool for an administrative position were asked the following:

> What resume criteria or factors do you use to develop an interview pool for an administrative position?

Results of Their Responses
Listed in Descending Order

Criteria and/or Positive Factors	*Percentage*
Proper and required certification, licenses, and education/degree	100
Experience that matches job description	96
Individual's match with district goals and programs	84
Professional/neat format and presentation	80
References	80

NOTE: Other factors listed in descending order include well-organized, well-rounded, recommendation of the district superintendent, in-district candidate, and shared personal information.

The same individuals responsible for developing interview pools were asked the following:

What résumé format and/or style characteristics do you view as negatives or detractors?

Results of Their Responses
Listed in Descending Order

Negative Résumé Format or Characteristics	*Percentage*
Disorganized and/or sloppy	100
Nontraditional paper or print color	84
Difficult-to-read or nontraditional print	72
Excessive length or wordiness	64
Nonrelevant information	36

NOTE: Other negative format characteristics include an unflattering picture and inappropriate or "cute" graphics.

Conclusions

When writing your résumé, include and emphasize the following:

- Certifications, licenses, education, and professional educational experiences that meet district goals, programs, needs, and so forth
- Appropriate references
- A brief, well-organized, and conservative format

Avoid the following:

- Inappropriate pictures and graphics
- Nontraditional paper, color, print, and so forth
- Wordiness and nonrelevant information

Sample Résumé for an Entry-Level Position

ROBERT GREEN
123 Lemon Drive
Hometown, IL 60400
Home: 815-123-4444

Education

Masters of Arts in Educational Administration, 1997, State University

Bachelor of Science in Industrial Technology, 1985, Northern University

Certificates

Illinois School Administrators Certificate (K-12), Type 75

Illinois Teacher Certificate (6-12) Industrial Technology

Illinois Teacher Certificate (K-12) Computer Technology

Work Experience

1995-present	Minooka High School, Minooka, IL Teacher: Industrial Technology Head Coach: Freshman Football
1992-1994	Channahon Junior High, Channahon, IL Teacher: Industrial Arts Head Coach: Baseball and Wrestling
1990-1992	Alleman High School, Rock Island, IL Dean of Student: Duties included student discipline, scheduling, staff evaluation, and curriculum development Teacher: Computer Literacy Head Varsity Coach: Baseball Assistant Varsity Coach: Football and Wrestling

Leadership Positions

Building Grievance Representative for the Minooka Teachers Organization

Chairman of Minooka School District Professional Development Committee

President of Lion's Club, Minooka Chapter

Secretary and Executive Board Member of the State University Chapter of Phi Delta Kappa

Organizations

Phi Delta Kappa

Lions Club

Association for Supervision and Curriculum Development

National Education Association

References

Dr. William Thomas, Superintendent, Minooka Schools	815-703-1000
Mr. Roger Clean, Principal, Minooka High School	815-703-1100
Dr. Mary Ann Peach, Principal, Channahon High School	815-660-5000
Mr. David Vlassic, Principal, Alleman High School	815-923-3900

Note: Written references available upon request

NOTE: Other appropriate headings that might apply are Published Works and Presentations, Honors, Personal Attributes, and Interests. For more information, visit the library. There are many books and booklets available that deal with letters of intent and résumés. Although most material is in the field of business, it can be easily adapted to school administration.

Examining the Style and Format of My Résumé

10 Items to Check

Circle Y (yes) or N (no) for each item:

1. Y or N The paper color is white, cream, or grey.
2. Y or N The print color is black or blue.
3. Y or N The paper is of a quality gauge or thickness.
4. Y or N The type is a standard and conservative print.
5. Y or N The print is easy to read.
6. Y or N The margins and type promote easy reading.
7. Y or N There are no inappropriate photos or graphics in this resume.
8. Y or N Topic areas begin with well-defined headings.
9. Y or N For each topic area, the information is organized in chronological order beginning with the most recent.
10. After examining this résumé, I find it is the following:
    - Y or N Neat
    - Y or N Well organized
    - Y or N Clear
    - Y or N Of appropriate length

Items circled Y (yes) are most preferred by superintendents, assistant superintendents, or others responsible for developing the interview pool. **Yes** responses are right on target in most districts!

For any item circled N (no), reread the preceding section. Make all desired corrections prior to finalization and distribution. If you choose to deviate from the norm, know why you have made this choice and be sure you wish to continue this practice.

Remember: *A good start is halfway there.*

Guide for Critiquing a Résumé

Applicant ______________________________

Score each area by circling only one rating on a 5-point scale, where 5 = high (excellent) and 1 = low (needs much improvement).

1. [5 4 3 2 1] The content is relevant to the desired position.
2. [5 4 3 2 1] The content is ordered well.
3. [5 4 3 2 1] The content is easy to understand.
4. [5 4 3 2 1] Education and proper certification are prominently positioned.
5. [5 4 3 2 1] Experience is prominently positioned.
6. [5 4 3 2 1] Format and presentation are neat.
7. [5 4 3 2 1] Presentation is well organized.
8. [5 4 3 2 1] Paper and print are a traditional color.
9. [5 4 3 2 1] Print is a simple font and easy to read.
10. [5 4 3 2 1] Length is appropriate (complete yet succinct).

Total all items circled. Write the sum here. ____

Divide the sum by 10. This is the overall rating. Write the rating here. ____

Write additional comments or suggestions here.

Case Problem: Will B. Mobile

Will B. Mobile has been the assistant principal at Paramount High School for the past 9 years. His last child has finally left the nest, and he and his wife have agreed to relocate to a warmer climate. For the first time in many years, Will finds he will be seeking a new administrative position. He is interested in either a position as an assistant or as a principal.

Mr. Mobile realizes that the first thing he must do is to compose a current résumé. He is unsure as to what he should include since he has not done this in a very long time. Help Will B. Mobile. List, in the order in which they should appear, the areas or topics you think he should include. Use the knowledge acquired in this section to help yourself. *Write your answer below.**

*See Appendix A for one suggested response.

3

Identifying Personal Qualities and Emphasizing Strengths

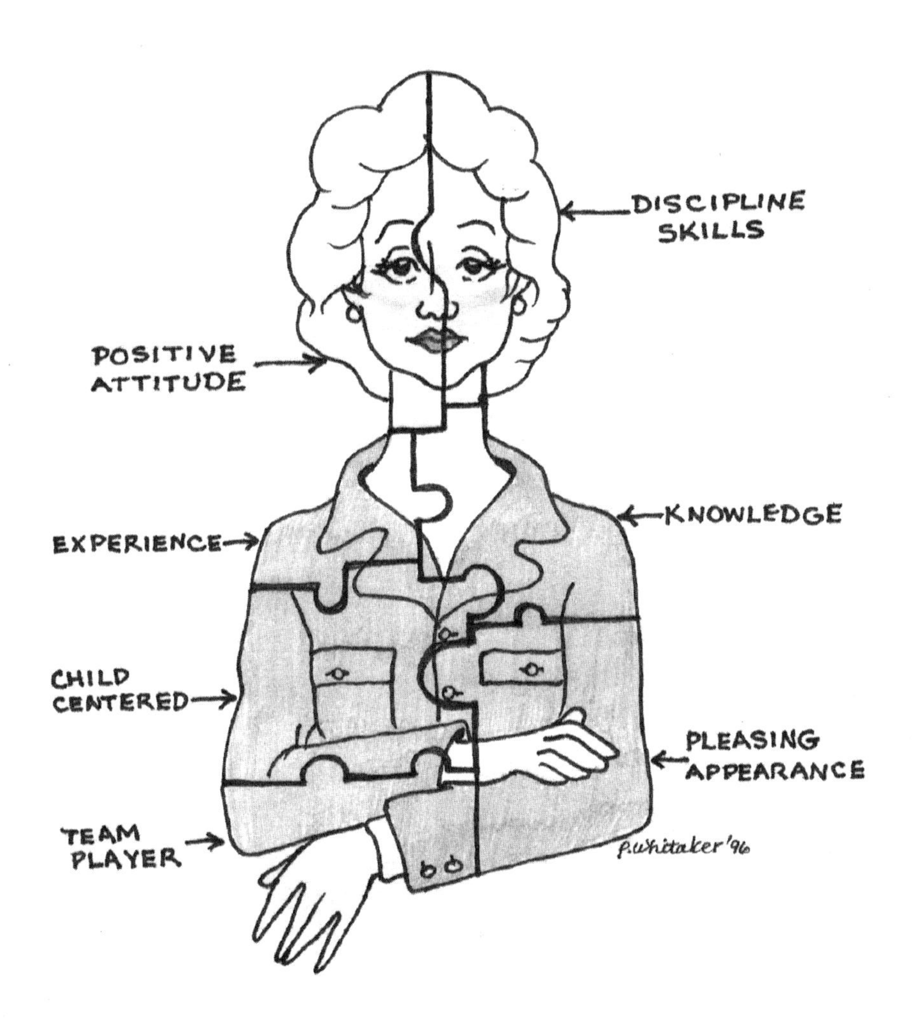

Identifying your personal qualities and the perceived strengths of men and women administrators helps you emphasize the right things in both the written documentation and the interview.

Steps to Identifying Personal and Perceived Strengths and Qualities

1. Use self-reflection to identify your own personal strengths and professional qualities.
2. Create a hierarchical list of these strengths and qualities.
3. Study what the survey data reveal about the perceived strengths of men and women who successfully secured their desired school administrative position.
4. By combining your list of personal strengths and the survey results of perceived gender strengths, develop a hierarchical list of strengths and qualities you wish to emphasize in correspondence and the interviews.

My Outstanding Professional Strengths and Qualities

Use this space to list your outstanding professional strengths and qualities.

Build your hierarchical list by writing the above strengths/qualities in descending order, with your most potent strength first, then your second, and so on.

What the Survey Data Reveal About Men's Strengths

What Qualities or Strengths Should I Emphasize?

People on selection committees who recently recommended hiring a man were asked to do the following:

> For the male you recommended for employment, list his three most outstanding qualities or strengths.

Male candidates who successfully secured a school administrative position were asked to do the following:

> List the three most outstanding qualities or strengths you possess that helped you get this position.

Results of Their Responses Listed in Descending Order

Males:

Perceived Qualities or Strengths	*Committees' View of Selected Males (%)*	*Successful Males' View of Self (%)*	*Total Percentage for All Responding*
Discipline skills favor firm discipline	72	78	75
Personality: positive, friendly, enthusiastic, and so forth	56	40	48
Knowledgeable	40	40	40
Experience	32	30	31
Public relations skills	24	26	25

NOTE: Other traits include good reputation, values children, values teachers, appearance, team player, values parent participation, and management skills.

Conclusions

Men seeking administrative positions should emphasize the following:

- Commitment to firm discipline and your discipline skills (If unfamiliar with current discipline beliefs and successful programs, review the literature.)
- Public relations experience and skills
- Your knowledge, experience, and positive attitude

What the Survey Data Reveal About Women's Strengths

What Qualities or Strengths Should I Emphasize?

People on selection committees who recently recommended hiring a woman were asked to do the following:

> For the female you recommended for employment, list her three most outstanding qualities or strengths.

Women candidates who successfully secured a school administrative position were asked to do the following:

> List the three most outstanding qualities or strengths you possess that helped you get this position.

Results of Their Responses Listed in Descending Order

Females:

Perceived Qualities or Strengths	*Committees' View of Selected Women (%)*	*Successful Females' View of Self (%)*	*Total Percentage for All Responding*
Child/student centered	48	53	50
Discipline skills favor firm discipline	48	36	42
Knowledgeable	40	36	38
Personality: positive, friendly, enthusiastic, and so forth	28	32	30
Experience	28	24	26

NOTE: Other traits include good reputation, values teachers, agrees with district educational philosophy, appearance, team player, values parent participation, gives concrete examples, and personal contacts.

Conclusions

Women seeking administrative positions should emphasize the following:

- Concern for children and their right to a quality education
- Commitment to firm discipline and your discipline skills (If unfamiliar with current discipline beliefs and successful programs, review the literature.)
- Your knowledge, experience, and positive attitude

Strengths That I Should Emphasize at the Interview

Combine your personal list of professional strengths and qualities with those strengths of your gender identified from the research data. *Write the top 10 in descending order below.*

1.

2.

3.

4.

5.

6.

7.

8.

9.

10.

Case Problem: Michelle La Creme

At the age of 30, Dr. Michelle La Creme is applying for her first principalship. She is eminently qualified, having earned an Ed.D. in school administration and having served as an assistant principal for 4 years. Yet she is apprehensive and lacks confidence because of her youth and limited classroom experience.

She comes to your office for guidance. She explains her reservations and fears. How would YOU help Dr. La Creme overcome her anxiety and prepare for this opportunity. Be specific. *Write your answer below.**

*See Appendix A for one suggested response.

4

Recognizing Personal Weaknesses and Defusing Fears

All people have personal and professional weaknesses. Recognizing and learning to cope with them is a mark of leadership. Also, selection committee members perceive that men or women administrators have inherent gender weaknesses. Even if these perceptions or fears are unfounded, they must be defused in order to secure the desired administrative position.

Steps to Identifying Personal and Perceived Weaknesses Associated With Gender

1. Use self-reflection to identify your own personal and professional weaknesses—for example, sloppy work habits, procrastination, or difficulty with the supervisory role.
2. Create a hierarchical list of these weaknesses.
3. Study what the survey data in this section suggest about the perceived weaknesses of men and women who successfully secured their desired school administrative position.
4. By combining your personal weakness list and the perceived gender weakness list, develop a hierarchical list of those you wish to combat and defuse in correspondence and the interviews.

My Weaknesses That Affect Professional Performance

Use this space to list those weaknesses that affect your professional performance.

Build your hierarchical list by writing the above weaknesses in descending order, with your most damaging fault first, then your second, and so on.

What the Survey Data Reveal About the Perceived Weaknesses of Women Administrators

What Concerns or Fears Should I Defuse?

People on selection committees who recently recommended hiring a woman were asked to do the following:

> For the woman you recommended for employment, list your three major concerns or fears.

Women candidates who successfully secured a school administration position were asked to do the following:

> Regarding yourself, list the three major concerns or fears of the selectors who hired you.

Results of Their Responses Listed in Descending Order

Females:

Perceived Concern or Fear	*Committees' View of Selected Women (%)*	*Successful Females' View of Self (%)*	*Total Percentage for All Responding*
Soft on discipline	64	76	70
Lack of experience	44	52	48
Fit existing team	52	28	40
Physical size, strength, and endurance	24	32	28
Emotionality	16	8	12

Conclusions

Women seeking administrative positions should address and defuse these concerns:

- Soft discipline
- Lack of experience
- Collegiality
- Endurance, strength, and inappropriate emotionality

NOTE: Other concerns include indiscriminate change agent, age, lack of knowledge of extracurricular issues, public speaking experience, and permanence (Will the candidate stay?).

What the Survey Data Reveal About the Perceived Weaknesses of Men Administrators

What Concerns or Fears Should I Defuse?

People on selection committees who recently recommended hiring a man were asked to do the following:

> For the man you recommended for employment, list your three major concerns or fears.

Male candidates who successfully secured a school administration position were asked to do the following:

> Regarding yourself, list the three major concerns or fears of the selectors who hired you.

Results of Their Responses Listed in Descending Order

Males:

Perceived Concern or Fear	*Committees' View of Selected Males (%)*	*Successful Males' View of Self (%)*	*Total Percentage for All Responding*
Lack of experience	72	76	74
Lack of knowledge	58	50	54
Bureaucratic	42	26	34
Soft on discipline	28	28	28
Will bring unwanted change	16	4	10

Conclusions

Men seeking administrative positions should address and defuse these concerns:

- Lack of experience and knowledge
- Lack of collegiality and democratic practices
- Soft discipline
- Indiscriminate change

NOTE: Other concerns include age, permanence, won't encourage parent participation, and doesn't value teachers' contributions and participation.

Weaknesses and Perceived Concerns That I Should Address and Defuse at the Interview

Combine your list of professional weaknesses with those perceived fears and concerns associated with your gender identified from the research data. *Write the top 10 in descending order below.*

1.

2.

3.

4.

5.

6.

7.

8.

9.

10.

Case Problem: Van Ity

Today is the big day. Mr. Van Ity has an interview with the superintendent and board members for the position of Director of Technology in his own district. He feels that this is only a formality since he has been unofficially acting in this capacity for almost a year. He doesn't believe the other finalist is a genuine threat, and he feels very confident.

Van Ity has prepared for this interview by rehearsing answers to probable questions and is comfortable with all of his responses except one. He is not sure how to answer the inevitable question about his weaknesses. His long-time friend and ex-boss, Keith Braghard, often cautioned him to "never admit a fault. It will only come back to bite you." Braghard had advised Van Ity to turn every conversation around so as to speak to his strengths rather than to his weaknesses. After mulling over the topic for the third time, Van finally decides to follow his friend's suggestion and refuse to discuss weaknesses or faults. Do you agree? Support your opinion with specifics. *Write your answer below.**

*See Appendix A for one suggested response.

5

Selection Committees

Learning which selection committees and which individuals favor hiring women or men for school administrative positions helps your presentation and confidence level during the interview.

Steps to Identifying a Favorable Selection Committee

1. Study the information provided by the survey data.
2. Read the current biases in the hiring practices of American organizations.
3. Retain knowledge for future reference. Remember, these are generalities.

What the Survey Data Reveal About Selection Committees

Who Selects Female Administrators?

An analysis of selection committees that recommended hiring female candidates suggests that these committees have specific and identifiable characteristics.

Committee Gender Composition

Committee with a majority of females	71%
Committee of equal gender	9%
Committee with a majority of males	20%

Individual Committee Members' Positions and the Committee Size

Position	***Percentage***
Teacher	42
Administrator	37
Superintendent	9
Other	12
Size of Committee	***Percentage***
Small (0–5)	9
Average (6–13)	60
Large (14–up)	31

Conclusions

Selection committees that favor women have these characteristics:

- Average to large in size
- Composed of a majority of teachers
- Composed of a majority of females

Who Selects Male Administrators?

An analysis of selection committees that recommended hiring male candidates suggests that these committees have specific and identifiable characteristics.

Committee Gender Composition

Committee with a majority of males	63%
Committee of equal gender	3%
Committee with a majority of females	34%

Individual Committee Members'
Positions and the Committee Size

Position	***Percentage***
Teacher	40
Administrator	37
Superintendent	15
Other	8
Size of Committee	***Percentage***
Small (0–5)	23
Average (6–13)	60
Large (14–up)	17

Conclusions

Selection committees that favor men have these characteristics:

- Average to small in size
- Composed of a majority of administrators
- Composed of a majority of males

Current Hiring Biases of American Organizations

A review of the current research regarding hiring practices of American organizations discloses some salient facts that you need to consider. The research confirms that hiring individuals and groups still have biases toward hiring certain individuals. School districts are among these organizations, and selection committees, superintendents, and school boards often make their hiring decisions with these identified biases. The most noteworthy are the following:

- Males are generally preferred to females.
- Attractive applicants are hired more often than unattractive applicants.
- When each candidate has high competence, the younger applicant is preferred to the older applicant.
- For positions of leadership, mature-faced individuals are preferred to baby-faced individuals (Cann, Siegfried, & Pearce, 1981; Haefner, 1977; Williams, 1992; Zebrowitz, Tenenbaum, & Goldstein, 1991).

Although you cannot change your gender, age, or facial maturity, you can do many things to improve your general attractiveness. Appropriate attire, acceptable weight and a heathy body, and good grooming are characteristics you control. It is worth your time and energy to care for yourself and thereby create an attractive appearance. For more information and helpful suggestions, refer to **Clothing Makes the Administrator** (Chapter 9)

Case Problem: Roll With the Punches

Mrs. Shirley Bend was waiting somewhat impatiently for her interview as one of three assistant principals at Evergreen High School. Suddenly, the door to the conference room opened, and Joe Firman, principal of the district's only junior high school, came forward, greeted her, and introduced himself. He explained that the selection committee was assembled and anxious to meet her. Mr. Firman assured her that there was no reason to be nervous because the committee members would do their best to make her feel welcome. Shirley was initially impressed by the cordial and professional start.

What Mrs. Bend saw as she entered the room made her heart sink. Four people sat on one side of a long rectangular table facing the lone straight-backed chair placed approximately 5 feet in front of the assembly—obviously, HER CHAIR. All conversation stopped as she approached. Although the committee members smiled, their appearance was quite intimidating.

After offering Shirley her chair, Mr. Firman introduced the other four members of the interview team. They were, from left to right, Tom Labors, teachers' union president; Marvel Ready, assistant principal; Dr. Jeff Smiles, principal; and Amanda Wiley, parent and community leader.

Mrs. Bend had prepared for this interview and knew the research indicated that small male-dominated committees most often recommend hiring men. What should Shirley Bend do? Can she turn this situation to her advantage? Does she stand a chance? *Write your answer below.**

*See Appendix A for one suggested response.

6

Women and Men Talking

Understanding that men and women have different communication purposes and styles gives you a powerful tool during the interview and contract negotiation session. Applying this knowledge will serve you well.

Steps to Follow When Communicating With the Opposite Gender During the Interview, Negotiations, and Later on the Job

1. Read what the current literature discloses about communication differences between men and women.

2. Practice. Start now and use the applicable prescriptions in your present position.

3. Apply the learned principles during the forthcoming interviews and initial negotiation.

What You Should Know and Do When Speaking to the Opposite Gender

Know That Most Often the Following Occur:

- When organizing perceptions, men look for differences, whereas women look for similarities.

  Rx for Women: **Include differences when making a point or arguing a position.**

  Rx for Men: **Include similarities when making a point or arguing a position.**

- Men take credit for team accomplishments and expect others to do likewise. Women verbally share triumphs with coworkers and refer to "our successes."

  Rx for Women: **Toot your own horn. Take rightful credit for accomplishments.**

  Rx for Men: **Don't forget to praise others along with yourself.**

- Men negotiate contracts and subsequent raises based on personal accomplishments and their unique value to the organization. Often, women use equity issues as the basis for bargaining.

  Rx for All: **List your virtues, accomplishments, and value when bargaining.**

- Men view frequent apologies as a sign of insincerity and/or manipulation. Women see apologies as indicators of empathy, good manners, or consideration of feelings.

  Rx for Women: **Monitor and, where necessary, censure your use of apologies.**

  Rx for Men: **Understand and accept the nature of women's apologies.**

- During verbal exchanges, men are more direct, information driven, time conscious, expedient, and focus on broad general topics. Women approach issues more slowly, focus on details to ensure a win-win conclusion, and are interested in both the informational and affective ramifications of the topic.

Rx for All: **Understand and tolerate these gender differences.**

- After heated debate or fierce confrontation, men more readily put "hard feelings on the shelf and go on" than do their women counterparts.

  Rx for Women: **Don't stew and waste your time ruminating. Move on!**

  Rx for Men: **Use verbal "bridges" to repair relationships after debate or confrontation.**

Case Problem: Think Before You Speak

Dr. Truman Gonzales is elated. He knows that he did well during his interview for the position of superintendent of Pleasant View School District. Dr. Gonzales is now scheduled to have "an off the record" dinner with the board members. The composition of the board is 5 women and 2 men. Three ethnic groups are represented. Truman is astute and realizes that he is still under scrutiny. He knows that a supposed informal meeting could make or break his changes of securing this position. Truman wants this job. If you were Dr. Gonzales's mentor and could give him only one piece of advice, what would you say? *Write your answer below.**

*See Appendix A for one suggested response.

Suggested Readings

Austin, N. K. (1996, March). The new job interview: Beyond the trick question. *Working Woman,* pp. 23-24.

Lakoff, R. T. (1990). *Talking power: The politics of language in our lives.* New York: Basic Books.

Mann, J. (1994). *The difference: Growing up female in America.* New York: Warner Books.

Nelson, M. B. (1994). *The stronger women get, the more men love football: Sexism and the American culture of sports.* New York: Harcourt Brace.

Tannen, D. (1994). *Talking 9 to 5. Women and men in the workplace: Language, sex and power.* New York: Avon Books.

Tannen, D. (1998). *Interviewing and recruiting process tips and techniques.* Atlanta: Consulting Resource Group.

7

Recognizing and Dealing With Harassment

Men and women must be able to recognize what constitutes real sexual harassment and learn how to behave if they experience this situation as a victim or an accused perpetrator. This will help you during the selection process as well as throughout your career.

Steps to Understanding and Handling Sexual Harassment

1. Read why you should become knowledgeable about sexual harassment.
2. Study the legal definition and types of sexual harassment.
3. Formulate a tentative response plan if you encounter sexual harassment in a prospective district.
4. Review key questions and answers.
5. Identify additional questions you have about sexual harassment and learn the answers.
6. Become familiar with inappropriate hiring questions. Understand that such questions might be an indication of the district's attitudes. Develop your own list of inappropriate and unacceptable questions.
7. Study the appropriate actions to take if you become a victim of sexual harassment.
8. Review the actions to take if an employee reports a case of harassment to you.
9. Learn the actions to take if you are unjustly accused of sexual harassment.
10. Peruse the suggested reading and information lists. Consider learning more.

Why You Should Become Acquainted With the Facts and Appropriate Actions When Dealing With Sexual Harassment

Today, American men and women are increasingly concerned about the existence of sexual harassment in the workplace. When seeking a new position as a school administrator, you need to understand the facts of sexual harassment, the appropriate actions to be taken if this situation arises, and the "track record" of your potential new organization.

Before you agree to accept a position in any school district, it is wise to investigate constituents' attitudes and past history in regard to harassment. In **Doing Your Homework Before the Interview** (Chapter 8), you will learn how important it is to gather information about the desired position and district prior to the interview. One reason to do your homework outlined in the next section is to determine the match between you and the new position. This practice holds true for sexual harassment. Questions to help you identify the desired district's position regarding harassment include these: Has the district experienced a sexual harassment action? How many? What occurred? Because of this action, what changes, if any, were made? What mechanism or safeguards are presently in place to equitably handle harassment charges in-house? Learning the answer to these questions and similar questions prior to signing a contract will help you determine if this is the place for you. You will also get an inkling for the value structure and code of ethics actually practiced in the prospective district. This could be a determining factor in accepting a position.

A second reason to become knowledgeable about this topic is the fact that, regardless of your gender, you could be a possible victim. All school administrators have peers and superordinates. With that a fact, the potential for becoming a victim of sexual harassment exists. You must know your rights and understand the appropriate and successful course of action to take if you are faced with this frightening and distasteful situation.

Finally, you need to learn about this subject if you accept a position as a supervisor. Anytime you are responsible for subordinates you become open to accusations (be they unfounded) of perpetration. These accusations may be direct, where a coworker accuses you of sexually harassing him or her, or indirect, where an individual might accuse you for not taking the correct action after sexual harassment has been reported to you. In either case, knowledge will help you control the situation and act correctly and successfully if the need arises.

How Should I Respond?

When considering the existence of potential or actual harassment within a prospective district, the question arises as to how you should respond. What will you do if you find evidence that harassment occurred or is suspected in the district you are considering joining? You should understand your feelings and beliefs and then develop a plan of action. Forethought will erase doubt and inappropriate behavior on your part.

Take action. After some self-reflection and an open discussion with your mentor, formulate your tentative response plan. *Jot down key steps here.*

Exactly What Is Gender or Sexual Harassment?

Although the media often cover stories of harassment, rarely is a conclusive definition of what constitutes genuine sexual harassment conveyed. To act professionally and effectively as a school administrator, you must understand the nature of harassment and have a clear concept of the necessary components. In its *Guidelines on Sexual Harassment,* the Equal Employment Opportunity Commission (EEOC, 1990) defines sexual harassment as follows:

> Unwelcome sexual advances, requests for sexual favors, and other verbal or physical conduct of a sexual nature constitute sexual harassment when (1) submission to such conduct is made either explicitly or implicitly a term or condition of an individual's employment, (2) submission to, or rejection of such conduct by an individual is used as the basis for employment decisions affecting such individuals, or (3) such conduct has the purpose or effect of unreasonably interfering with an individual's work performance or creating an intimidating, hostile, or offensive working environment. (unpaginated)

More specifically, there are two major categories of sexual harassment. They are *quid pro quo* and *condition of work* (Baxter, 1985).

Quid pro quo sexual harassment is defined by the more or less explicit exchange. Exchange is *where the individual must comply sexually or forfeit any employment benefit.* In this case, the exchange may be anything but subtle and may be verbalized euphemistically. This form of harassment involves a perpetrator who has a position of authority and power and a subordinate victim, and usually takes one of these three forms:

1. The individual denies an unwanted sexual advance and forfeits an employment opportunity. This is the clearest of all situations and the easiest to recognize. The pattern is sexual advance, noncompliance, and then employment retaliation.
   Examples:

- You need to sleep with me if you want the promotion.
- Be "nice" if you want me to recommend you.
- You could be transferred if you don't "give at the office."

2. The individual complies with unwanted sexual advances for promises of advancement on the job and the benefits do not materialize. This situation is more complex. Research suggests that those who do comply often experience broken promises and an exchange of bad faith. The key issue here is whether or not compliance was coerced by economic threat or promise. In this case, the injury of sexual harassment occurs because the individual is placed in a position of having to choose between unwanted sex and employment benefits.
   Examples:

   - He worked very "hard" on the weekends at the principal's cabin to be selected as her new assistant, and then she gave the job to someone else.
   - Did she think sleeping with him would get her the principalship?

3. The individual complies with unwanted sexual conditions and receives employment advantages over those who refuse. This situation implies that the compliant individual lacks competence and the proper qualifications.
   Examples:

   - She got the grant on her back.
   - I heard he slept his way to the top.

The second major category of sexual harassment is condition of work. This form is less clear but more pervasive in all work situations. In a television special, *Final Take: Sexual Harassment,* which aired in May 1996 on the Lifetime Television Network, it was pointed out that only 5% of sexual harassment suits were quid pro quo, whereas the other 95% were filed because of a hostile environment.

In this case, sexual harassment simply makes the work environment unbearable. Unwanted sexual advances reoccur and become a daily part of the work life. Perpetrators may be superordinates or peers, and victims are usually subordinates or peers. Individuals are coerced into tolerating unwanted and inappropriate advances and behaviors. These cases do not include the notion of exchange of sexual favors for a promise for employment advancement or threat of loss of benefits. The courts have ruled that unwanted sexual advances in the category of condition of work or "hostile environment" include unwanted touches (blatant or "accidental"), visual stripping, sexually suggestive comments, crude and vulgar speech (this includes off-color jokes), and invasion of personal space (MacKinnon, 1992).

It should be noted that the growing body of information regarding harassment is constantly changing. Laws are being challenged. As an administrator, you must stay abreast of court case decisions and adjust accordingly.

Separating Fact From Fiction: Questions and Answers About Sexual Harassment

The following questions and answers about sexual harassment should help you as you seek a position and throughout your tenure as a school administrator.

Is sexual harassment illegal?

Yes. It is a form of sexual discrimination, and therefore, in violation of Title VII of the 1964 Civil Rights Act, Title IX of the 1972 Education Amendments, and the Civil Rights Act of 1991.

Does sexual harassment include all unwanted sexual behavior?

Yes. This includes any offensive or undesirable conduct not solicited or encouraged by the worker. This constitutes a form of sexual discrimination and is illegal.

Must coercion exist for a situation to be deemed sexual harassment?

Yes. Either actual or implied coercion must be present for sexual harassment to exist.

Who can be a victim or a perpetrator of sexual harassment?

Anyone in the workplace is a potential perpetrator or victim. Men may harass women and vice versa. Women may harass other women, and men may harass other men. Bosses, peers, and subordinates may sexually harass any of their coworkers. Sexual harassment crosses all lines of gender, class, and race.

Where does sexual harassment occur?

Sexual harassment may occur at work or away from the workplace. It may even occur on a date if the parties share a common workplace (Eskenazi & Gallen, 1991).

Is sexual harassment that pervasive?

Yes. It is occurring today at an alarming rate. A most conservative estimate shows that at least 42% of all women will experience some form of harassment during their employment lives. Statistics for men are more sketchy because, as the research shows, men are less likely than women to report incidences of harassment. Also, it should be noted that, to date, there are fewer females in positions of power where they might abuse the situation and become perpetrators against their male peers and subordinates.

Why are so many incidences of sexual harassment not reported?

Anita Hill (1991) lists five reasons:

- Unwillingness to deal with the expected consequences. The individual knows the results will be traumatic and chooses not to rock the boat.
- Self-blame
- Blackmail or threats from bosses or coworkers
- A sense of powerlessness in the workplace
- A belief that "telling" is shameful and will result in the loss of job, emotional devastation, and lack of support

What is Post-traumatic Stress Disorder (PTSD), and how is it related to harassment?

Dr. Dennis R. Pollack, nationally recognized vocational psychologist, cites the American Psychiatric Association's (1994) *Diagnostic and Statistical Manual–IV* and explains PTSD in lay terms as follows:

> Post-traumatic stress occurs when an individual is exposed to a traumatic event in which the individual experienced, witnessed, or was confronted with an event or events that involved actual or threatened death or serious injury or a threat to the physical integrity of self or others. The person's response involved intense fears, helplessness, or horror.
>
> The traumatic event is persistently reexperienced in one of more of the following ways.
>
> - The individual experiences recurrent and intrusive distressing recollections of the events, including images, thoughts, or perceptions.
> - The individual may have distressing dreams of the event.
> - The individual may feel as if the traumatic event was reoccurring.
> - There is intense psychological distress at exposure to internal or external cues that symbolize or resemble an aspect of the traumatic event.
> - There is physiological reactivity upon exposure to internal or external cues that symbolize or resemble an aspect of the traumatic events.
>
> There is persistent avoidance of stimuli associated with the trauma and numbing of general responsiveness. These may include efforts to avoid thoughts, feelings, or conversations associated with the trauma. There are efforts to avoid activities, places,

or people that arouse recollections of the traumatic event. There is an inability to recall significant aspects of the traumatic event. There is a diminished interest or participation in cherished activities. There is a feeling of detachment or estrangement from others. There is restricted range of emotions. There is a sense of foreshortened future.

There are symptoms of increase autonomic arousal. These include difficulty falling or staying asleep. There is irritability or outbursts of anger. There is difficulty concentrating. The person may be hypervigilant. There is an exaggerated startle response.

We can all identify with some traumatic event in our life—the death of a loved one, a mugging, an auto accident, and so forth. Any of these occurrences might precipitate PTSD in vulnerable people. The same might be said of sexual harassment. It is possible to suffer PTSD after involvement or experience with harassment. Individuals must be aware of this possibility and be willing to seek professional help if symptoms arise. (D. Pollack, personal communication, June 1, 1998)

Who defines unwanted sexual advances?

Although the EEOC guidelines seem clear on the issue of sexual harassment, the question of who defines unwanted sexual advances is less definitive. Unwanted sexual advances are those advances perceived as undesirable by the supposed victim. These interpretations can vary greatly between individuals. One person might view frequent positive comments regarding his or her appearance as compliments, whereas another person might view such statements as unwanted sexual advances.

Individual court rulings have not been uniform in their outcomes. No guidelines are available as to what is reasonable or what is unreasonable when defining unwanted sexual advances. Rather, interpretation of what is regarded as unwanted sexual advances is determined on a case-by-case basis.

Unanswered Questions

Because the questions just addressed are not inclusive, you probably have several more questions that need answering. *List those questions here.*

Finding the Answers

To find the answers to these new questions, consult the following sources:

- The information agencies listed in Appendix B
- Your mentor
- A local school attorney
- A professor of Educational Administration or School Law

Inappropriate Hiring Questions

You do know that all questions posed on applications and at interviews give you an insight of the organization and/or the questioner. The type of questions asked by a district says much about its own beliefs and practices. Questions posed on applications and at interviews will help you determine if your new employers value and respect individuals, and if they will value and respect you. Inappropriate hiring questions should indicate to you that the position you are considering is not as desirable as you previously believed. Perhaps this is a position you need to reject.

Examples of inappropriate hiring questions:

How do you feel about men/women in positions of authority?

Are you happy in your personal life?

What is your age, gender, or race?

Do you regularly attend church? What church do you attend?

Do you have a significant other?

Although these types of questions are usually posed more subtly, elements of the above blatant examples are implied.

List your own examples. Remember, these are hypothetical questions that you would find offensive and/or illegal.

Your Response to Inappropriate Hiring Questions

How will you respond to inappropriate hiring questions? What if they appear on an application? What if they are posed during the interview process?

Take action. Use self-reflection and discuss possible responses with your mentor. Responses could range from withdrawing your application to ignoring the indication. *Jot down possible responses here.*

After You Accept the Position

It is possible that after you accept the position and begin working, you will encounter some form or situation of sexual harassment. Know that there are some effective actions you might take to deal correctly with the problem. Some of these are listed below.

Appropriate Actions to Take When You Are the Victim of Harassment

If you are a victim of sexual harassment, the following recommended steps to deal with this situation will bring positive results.

- Directly advise your harasser that the attention is unwanted, and you want that person to desist.
- Document events. Keep a written record of what happened, where and when it happened, any witnesses, your response, and who you told and what you said after the encounter.
- Attempt to find out if your harasser has harassed others.
- Report the incident to your supervisor and ask the supervisor to see to it that the harassment is stopped.
- Formally file a written report through the district's internal grievance system or guidelines identified in its policy guide.
- If the harassment does not stop after the previous steps are taken, on the advice of counsel take action outside the district. You may file a charge with the EEOC and/or file a lawsuit under Title VII, file a private monetary damages tort, or file a suit of sexual discrimination under your state's law. It is best to consult your lawyer before taking action (Eskenazi & Gallen, 1992).
- Find support. Consult the list of support resources provided in Appendix B. These groups may direct you to local help.

Appropriate Actions to Take If an Employee Reports a Case of Sexual Harassment to You

As a school administrator, you periodically will have subordinates or peers turn to you for guidance and protection. This is possible in both alleged and actual sexual harassment cases. Some guidelines when dealing with such a situation are the following:

- Handle the matter seriously.
- Remain objective, yet treat the possible victim with respect.
- Employ standards of professional confidentiality.
- Gather all available pertinent information. Keep a diary of the incidents. It is important that you notify the harasser of your objection to that person's behavior.
- Immediately report the incident to your superior and, if appropriate, seek guidance from the district's legal counsel. Follow the advice given.
- Document all subsequent actions.
- Follow through to resolution.

Appropriate Actions to Take If Unjustly Accused of Committing Sexual Harassment

Any unfair accusation is traumatizing. In a position of authority you are a possible target of unfounded and false accusations. If you are unjustly accused of being a perpetrator of sexual harassment, there are several steps you should take to defend yourself.

- Remain calm, yet alert. A hot temper or ambivalence are your enemy at this time.
- The best defense is innocence. Your positive past performance and daily demeanor will speak well for you when unjustly accused.
- You need help. Ask for it. Immediately report any charge of sexual harassment to your superior and seek counsel from the school attorney.
- Follow the advice of your superiors and counsel. Stick to the book and follow prescribed procedure.
- Take appropriate (nonvindictive) action.

Case Problem: Arndt Sure

Arndt Sure is confused! Today, he had a working lunch with Ginger DeVamp, Principal of Apple Orchard Elementary School. Ginger was new to the district, and it was not the first time she had asked for his help. With 14 years' experience as an elementary principal in the district, Arndt felt obliged to help and was flattered that she recognized his expertise. But lunch did not go well.

Thinking back on the experience, Arndt could remember a number of incidents that made him, a happily married man, very uncomfortable. Ginger was wearing a sheer blouse, and it was obvious that she wasn't wearing a bra. Several times she changed the conversation to compliment his appearance, and twice her leg brushed against his as they talked and ate.

What was going on? Was this a series of accidents or mere coincidence? Was it innocent and just Ginger's personality? Or was this a deliberate seduction, something he certainly did not court or want? If it was the latter, did Ginger's behavior constitute sexual harassment? Or not? Help Arndt Sure. Answer his questions. If this was a form of sexual harassment, what could and should Arndt Sure do? *Write your answer below.**

*See Appendix A for one suggested response.

8

Doing Your Homework Before the Interview

Doing your homework before the interview is one of the most critical activities you can do to secure the desired position. Knowing what to ask when invited to interview, learning about the district and position prior to the interview, and identifying good sources of information will prepare you for the interview. If possible, consider doing your homework about the position before you apply.

Steps for Preparation Prior to the Interview

1. Engage in self-reflection or solitary brainstorming to identify sources of information and methods to learn about the desired position prior to the interview. List your thoughts.
2. Confer with trusted colleagues and get their recommendations for techniques and sources of information about the position and district. Summarize their suggestions.
3. Carefully review the sections on "big" and "match" questions and mentally apply them to your situation.
4. Study the provided techniques and sources of information to learn about the position prior to the interview. Take the warnings seriously.
5. Read and apply the survey data results. Include these in the arsenal of practices you use prior to the interview.

How to Learn About the Position and the District Before the Interview

Brainstorm ways to learn about the position and district before the interview. List your ideas below. Number your choices in descending order, with 1 being most effective, and so on.

Query Trusted Colleagues

List 5 techniques or sources of information suggested by your colleagues to learn about the position and district.

1.

2.

3.

4.

5.

Questions You Should Ask When Invited to Interview

When that phone call happens, ask the contact person these questions:

By whom, when, and where will you be interviewed?

The names and positions of the interviewers are most helpful when preparing potential questions and answers.

Knowledge of when and where helps you feel more secure and in control.

Knowledge of time and place ensures punctuality.

What materials would the district like you to bring to the interview?

If you have a portfolio, it is acceptable to ask if it is appropriate to bring it at this time. Be prepared to leave all materials with the interviewers for a reasonable time. Remember, "less can be more."

Avoid bringing obsolete material that will only date you. Cute thank-you notes, poor-quality copies, and unrelated materials are detrimental.

How does the initial interview fit into the total search process?

Related questions important to your planning might include these:

- Are subsequent interviews planned?
- Are interviewees' names still confidential?
- When will references be checked?
- Will there be site visits?
- What is the projected timetable for all activities?

Doing Your Homework About the Position, School, and District Prior to the Interview

"Big" Questions

"Big" questions are usually those issues that a district uses itself to create a profile for the ideal candidate. They are the foundation for judging you and your competition. Foremost among these questions are the following:

- Where is the district or school now? Where would it like to be in the next several years?
- What major issues (positives and negatives) will the district or school confront during the next several years?
- What will the community, my superordinates, and my staff expect me to do about the aforementioned issues? What is my primary role in the next several years?
- What specific skills, knowledge, and experience must I bring to this position?
- What personal and professional characteristics are absolutely critical to be a successful leader in this community?

"Match" Questions

"Match" questions will vary from person to person and from situation to situation. They are personal and depend on one's vision, values, goals, and personal preferences. A serious and astute candidate should ask questions PRIOR TO the interview to determine if there is a good fit or match between the district or school and oneself. Does this position fulfill my aspirations, desires, and preferences? Are the required duties the kind of tasks I enjoy? Would I feel comfortable here? Do the pros outweigh the cons? Is this a great place for me?

For example, you are searching for your first superintendency, and there are potential positions in District A and District B. One possible match question might be as follows: Is the experience in District A better for me at this time in my career than the desirable salary of District B? Only you can determine meaningful match questions, weigh the importance, and evaluate responses.

Often, match questions are answered as you discover the answers to the big questions. However, you must use self-reflection while doing your homework to bring this into focus. If any crucial match questions are not answered indirectly as just suggested, ask them directly.

Five Powerful Techniques and Sources of Information

Although this is but a partial list of available techniques and sources of information, it will provide you with a superior jumping-off point. You should use these prior to the interview and, if feasible, seriously consider using them before applying. Why waste your valuable time applying for a position that is not right for you?

- **Acquire objective data.** The district itself, the state department of education, and the public library are excellent sources of objective data. Many agencies, organizations, and districts have available on-line computer information sites. These are easily and anonymously accessed. You can gather current demographic statistics for the community, district, and school; learn the present salaries of district employees; examine mission and vision statements; peruse new parent packets, public relations brochures, and the district's State Report Card, and so forth.

  Two cautions. First, be selective when gathering this material. There is a mountain of available information and only limited time. Second, don't overdo it during the interview. After doing your homework you will probably know more about the district than those who will interview you. Excessive "data dropping" can be a turnoff.

- **Get assistance from your network.** Your local university contacts, professional organizations and members, Educational Service Center specialists, clubs, and so forth are excellent sources of information.

Note. These are hearsay sources, and so you must go public with your aspirations to tap them.

- **Speak with personal contacts associated with the district (and school).** It is not considered proper protocol to speak with interviewers and possible superordinates before the interview. However, you are free to speak confidentially with current district staff or residents not serving on the search or selection committee.

  Note. These people provide only subjective opinions and are usually strongly vested in the organization. Treat this information with extreme caution. Remember, these people speak not only with you but with others.

- **Contact the person who currently holds the position you want** (but do so *only* if the separation is amenable). Occasionally, the person who is being replaced (retiring or moving up or on) will speak with you. This is a legitimate source of information, provided that person is not involved in the hiring process. This technique requires a considerable amount of bravery and daring. Often, you must call a stranger and convince that person to share information with you.

  Two cautions. First, this technique could backfire if major players feel it is inappropriate. Second, the information will be highly subjective.

- **Visit the community.** If time and money permit, a visit to the district prior to the interview is invaluable. This technique could answer many of your match questions. Try to forget about the job opportunity that brings you to the community. Think like a prospective resident. Drive around and get the feel of the locale. Would you (and your family) feel this is a good place to live? Does the community have the church, parks, housing, library, stores, and so on that you prefer and that match your lifestyle? Speak to the people, the unofficial greeters—a realtor, policeman, store clerk, librarian, service station attendant. Will you (and your family) eventually feel welcome and belong (Kremer, 1996)?

What Survey Data Reveal About Helpful Practices Before the Interview

What Should I Know and Do Before the Interview?

Candidates who recently secured an administrative position were asked the following:

> What advice would you give a friend before he or she interviewed for an administrative position?

Results of Their Responses
Listed in Descending Order

Advice Given	*Percentage*
Do your homework on the district and job requirements	94
Be sincere/truthful (co-opt negatives)	90
Be yourself	80
Emphasize your assets	72
Prepare answers to hypothetical questions with potential responses	64

NOTE: Other responses include dress appropriately, mention your educational philosophy, use proven speaking techniques (body language, humor, etc.), and ask intelligent questions.

Conclusions

Before you interview, do the following:

- Obtain specific information.
- Be “yourself” (i.e., personable and calm with a pleasant public image).
- Determine your assets and emphasize your strengths.
- Engage in self-examination.
- Ask the assistance of others.
- Practice with your mentor.

Case Problem: Start With a Plan

Mr. M. T. Head has just made a major life decision. As a recently divorced single parent with custody of his only daughter, M.T. has decided to relocate to a new part of the state and begin again. He is presently employed as the principal at Apex Elementary School. He has successfully served in that capacity for 6 years but believes he would like to raise his child in a more rural environment than where he is presently located. He wants to put the past behind him and give his daughter and himself a fresh start.

Mr. M. T. Head is usually a methodical person who rarely leaves anything to chance. Under the personal stress, he finds it difficult to concentrate on any project, let alone his own needs and desires. He just knows that his first step is to learn more about potential locations and the present job market for elementary school administrators in qualifying areas. M. T. fervently believes he must start with a plan, but he can't formulate the first step—if only he had a place to start. Help M. T. Head begin his search. What are some of the actions you would recommend? *Write your answer below.**

*See Appendix A for one suggested response.

9

Clothing Makes the Administrator

Knowing what attire is perceived as most acceptable by selection committees is helpful when choosing your interview wardrobe.

Steps to Take When Selecting Your Interview Wardrobe

1. Study what the survey data reveal about the clothing preferences of selection committees and district key players.

2. If necessary, consider using this information to spruce up your wardrobe. The investment of funds will pay excellent dividends.

What the Survey Data Reveal About Interview Clothing

What Should Women Wear?

Information on this topic was gathered from school districts that hired female administrators and from the successful women themselves.

Demographics of Surveyed Districts

Level	*Percentage*
Elementary school	54
Middle/Junior high school	12
High school	18
Central office	16
Socioeconomic Status (SES)	***Percentage***
Low to low-middle	12
Middle	46
High-middle to high	42

NOTE: All grade and SES levels were represented in the survey.

Actual Attire and District Descriptors
for Successful Women

Attire	*Percentage*
Blue suit	54
Blue dress	4
Total	58
Tan or grey suit	26
Tan or grey dress	6
Total	32
Other (nontraditional) suit	6
Other (nontraditional) dress	4
Total	10
Four Descriptors Most Often Used by Districts to Describe Successful Women	*Percentage*
Neat/well-groomed	69
Clean/crisp/tailored	52
Professional	28
Conservative	6

Conclusion

Women should wear a **blue suit** for the interview. Clothing should be neatly pressed, hair clean and neatly groomed, and nails sport length and neat. Note that *no successful women wore slacks.*

What Should Men Wear?

Information on this topic was gathered from school districts that hired male administrators and from the successful men themselves.

Actual Attire and District Descriptors
for Successful Men

Attire	*Percentage*
Dark suit	69
Dark sport coat and slacks	5
Total	74
Light-colored suit/sport coat	23
Other	3
Total	26
Four Descriptors Most Often Used by Districts to Describe Successful Men	*Percentage*
Neat/well-groomed	69
Professional	54
Appropriate	28
Conservative	6

Conclusion

Men should wear a **conservative, dark suit** to the interview.

Case Problem: Barry Tight

Barry Tight took the tan-and-grey plaid sport coat from the closet so that he would remember to drop it off at the cleaners. He would need it next Wednesday morning for his interview as principal at the middle school. Barry knew he was ready for this new assignment and looked forward to the interview. As a high school assistant principal he had been responsible for student discipline and the academic progress of the freshman class. He enjoyed his job and had done well. But he needed to move on, especially now with his wife, Shela, at home caring for their two preschool children. They needed the added income, and this new position seemed perfect for him.

Barry took a second look at the casual jacket in his hand. He understood that convention dictated that he should wear a dark suit, but this was the best sport coat he owned. The last suit he'd bought was now 7 years old, a little tight, and out of date. Yes, the plaid jacket with charcoal slacks, white shirt, and a conservative tie was his best choice. It would have to do. He would buy a couple of new suits if he got the job. Respond to Barry Tight's decision. How would you advise him to proceed? *Write your answer below.**

*See Appendix A for one suggested response.

10

Most Often Asked Interview Questions

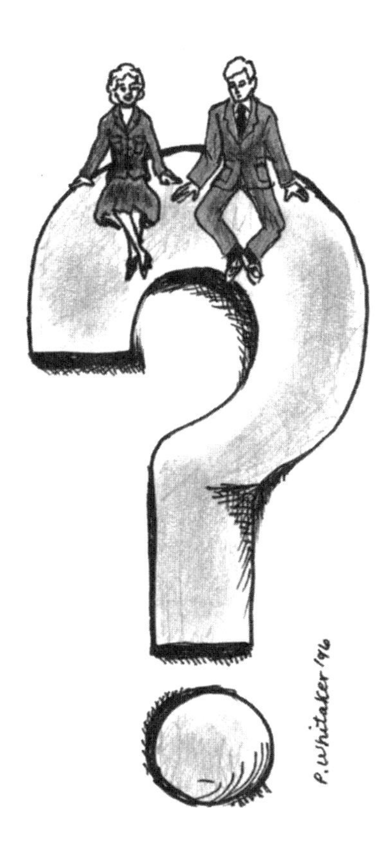

Learning the most often asked interview questions and then rehearsing your answers to these and other questions that are unique to the desired position will ensure that your interview is successful.

Steps to Preparing Answers to Often Asked Interview Questions

1. Read the suggestions for preparing your responses to interview questions.
2. Brainstorm your own prioritized list of predictable interview questions.
3. Study what the survey data identify as the most often discussed interview topics or issues.
4. Using the previous lists, create several questions and answers for the identified topics.
5. Prepare your answers to frequently asked interview questions.
6. Verbally practice your responses with your mentor. Videotaping a mock interview is most helpful. If at all possible, use this technique!

Preparation

When you prepare responses to interview questions, you must consider the content of your response and the delivery. Advanced preparation will help you approach interviews with more personal control and less nervousness.

The Content. Although you don't want to memorize word-for-word your responses to anticipated questions, you should fix in your mind the main points you want to emphasize, keeping in mind what you have learned about the district, its interests, and priorities.

Refer to your mental outline as the interview proceeds. This stored information will give you confidence and keep you focused on the question posed. If you forget a point or two as you are responding to an anticipated question, let it go. Don't dwell on the individual point. No one, except you, knows what you considered a complete and ideal answer. A missed point will not determine your overall performance unless you become compulsive and refuse to move forward.

Mary Heiberger and Julia Vick (1992) suggest, "Prepared with the knowledge of what you wish to discuss, you can use even unexpected questions that come your way as an opportunity to discuss the ideas you wish to convey" (p. 113)

Delivery. To polish your delivery, there is no substitute for practice and honest, positive criticism. This is where your mentor can be very helpful. Ask your mentor to participate in a mock interview with you as the candidate and your mentor as interviewer. Videotape the session. Later, the two of you should candidly critique your body language, tone, verbal quality, and so forth. Welcome and apply the feedback to polish your performance.

If the suggested exercise is not feasible, another alternative is your local college or university. Many campus career planning and placement centers offer practice interview sessions. Take advantage of this service to improve your delivery.

Identifying the Most Often Asked Interview Questions

Brainstorm a list of most often asked interview questions or topics. What would you ask if you were on a selection committee? Prioritize and rank your list in descending order. *Write and number your responses here.*

What the Survey Data Reveal Are the Most Often Discussed Interview Topics or Issues

The 10 most often discussed topics or issues in school administration interviews are the following:

1. Your personal history and accomplishments including preparation and experience
2. Your leadership style and educational philosophy with practical examples
3. Your vision of the role of parents, community, and local business in the school (district)
4. Your discipline philosophy with real-life examples
5. The strengths you bring to this position
6. The weaknesses you bring to the position
7. Your attitudes toward special and gifted education
8. Your attitudes and style when working with teachers
9. How you institute change
10. Your knowledge and experience of curriculum

EXERCISE 1

Formulating My Own List of Questions and Answers

Use the brainstorming and survey lists to create several questions and answers for the topics and issues identified. *Write these here.*

EXERCISE 2

Preparing My Answers to Frequently Asked Interview Questions

Jot down notes, outline, or list points you wish to include when discussing the following questions:

- Tell us a little about yourself.

- How would you describe your leadership style?

- How do you plan to include parents in their child's education and school?

- Give us some examples of actions you have taken that reflects your discipline philosophy.

- What strengths do you bring to this position?

- What are your weaknesses?

- Explain your position on special education and gifted education.

- Describe your style when working with teachers.

- How have you gone about bringing change to a school (district) in the past?

- Describe three successful educational programs you have implemented.

Do You Have Any Questions for Us?

One question not addressed in the survey is the most often asked concluding question. Most interviews end with "Is there anything you would like to ask us? or "Do you have any questions for us?" Don't underestimate the importance of this question. Your reply will usually be the last impression the selection committee has of you. This question might determine a selection committee's positive or negative recommendation.

So, how should you answer this question? The right response is *always* "yes." A "no" response only suggests that you are uninformed or uninterested. Prepare a few questions in advance but be sure to include several questions that are a response to what you have learned to be significant from the interview itself (Heiberger & Vick, 1992). By tying your questions to the original interview topics your questions become timely and lively rather than formulaic.

Two examples of questions that piggyback off the initial selection committee questions might be the following:

- Twice during the interview the selection committee queries your understanding and feelings about portfolios. Obviously, they are interested in initiating, continuing, or expanding a use of portfolios in the classroom. A potential pertinent question from you at the conclusion of the interview might be this: "I was impressed with your interest in portfolios. Tell me if you have instituted the use of portfolios as an alternative form of assessment? Where are you in the implementation phase?"
- While interviewing for the position of principal you are asked about your familiarity and experience with a NO-TOLERANCE POLICY FOR DRUGS AND GANGS. In this case, you might pose these concluding questions: "You mentioned that you were concerned about drugs and gangs in the schools. What needs does the district have in this area? What would you like to see happen in the school? How do you envision the principal proceeding?"

Questions about salary or benefits are not appropriate at this time. Save these questions until you are offered the position.

Case Problem: Smelling Like a Rose

Dr. Rose Thomas-Brown was cruising through the many interview questions posed to her over the past 40 minutes. She reflected briefly on how happy she was that she had done her homework on the district and had prepared her answers to so many of the anticipated questions. She was well-qualified for the position of Assistant Superintendent of Personnel and her preparation prior to the interview helped her express herself clearly and represent herself well.

Then it happened. Mrs. Katchem, selection committee member representing the business community asked, "Tell us about the last unrelated-to-education nonfiction book you read." What kind of question was that? What did Rose's reading habits have to do with her administrative abilities? Was this a trap, or did it have some kind of meaning that Dr. Thomas-Brown didn't understand? Rose's mind was in turmoil, and she felt flustered and unprepared.

Pretend you are Rose. How would you answer? What speaking techniques would you use? Why would you respond in this way? *Write your answer below.**

*See Appendix A for one suggested response.

11

Negotiating Your Contract Successfully

Learn the principles and the art of power negotiating. Learn the critical issues to be addressed when negotiating your administrative contract. This will improve your level of success and positively affect your working conditions for as long as you choose to remain in the position.

Steps to Negotiating a Successful Contract for Your New Position

1. Study what the survey data identify as important topics to address when negotiating an initial contract.
2. Study the data results to learn how to successfully discuss and negotiate starting salary.
3. Learn from business by reading the 12 points necessary to follow when engaged in the act of power negotiations. Begin practicing these techniques in all future negotiations so as to feel comfortable when you negotiate the all-important contract.

What the Survey Data Reveal About Negotiating an Administrative Contract

What Should I Address When Negotiating My Contract

The following question was posed to practicing administrators who had a minimum of 4 years' experience:

> What would you advise a friend to address when negotiating a new contract with your district?

Results of Their Responses
Listed in Descending Order

Issue	*Percentage*
Starting salary	100
Entry level, experience level, and raises	100
Length of contract and security	92
Benefits (insurance, bonuses, merit pay)	84
Professional development (time and money)	56

NOTE: Other issues include travel reimbursement, promotion opportunities, and evaluation procedures.

The same practicing administrators were asked the following:

> What advice would you give a friend when negotiating starting salary in your district?

Results of Their Responses
Listed in Descending Order

Topic	*Percentage*
Know and discuss range and issues that affect placement on the salary scale	72
Know, and if advantageous, discuss salaries and qualifications of present administrator(s)	64
Discuss (sell) your uniqueness, qualifications, and advantageous characteristics	56
Initially ask for a high salary and then be prepared to compromise	32
While negotiating, maintain a positive, firm, and friendly demeanor	3

NOTE: Other topics include verbal review, reiteration, summarization of agreed-on terms, and the meticulous review and correction of all errors in the written contract prior to signing.

Conclusions

Positive actions you should use when negotiating your initial contract:

- Do your homework prior to negotiating
- Bring a list of negotiating points
- Negotiate positively: be friendly, firm, and reasonable
- Make notes during negotiations and then reiterate and summarize agreed-on points
- Request that all items be included in the written contract
- Review and correct all errors in the written contract prior to signing

Learning From Business: 12 Points to Remember When Engaging in Power Negotiations

"Win-win" settlements are usually a myth in the real world. Most often, both parties want opposite resolution on a given point. Instead of striving for "win-win," use power negotiating. Power negotiating shows you how to win but lets the other person *feel* as if he or she has won.

Like a game of chess, **negotiations are "played" with strategic moves called gambits.** Beginning gambits get the game started in your direction. All future moves are dependent on quality beginning gambits. Middle gambits keep it moving in your favor or direction. Ending gambits prepare you to make the deal you desire.

Ask for more than you expect to get. This gambit achieves two purposes: It increases your perceived value and prevents deadlock. Experienced negotiators realize that first offers seem extreme but are only the beginning or starting point. They expect to work toward an agreement that both parties can accept.

Don't say yes to the first offer. If you agree to the first offer, your opposition will wonder if he or she could have done better or worry that something must be wrong. He or she will feel cheated or mistrust your developing relationship.

React with shock and surprise to the opposition's proposals. Physically flinch. This is crucial, as most people believe that they can see more than they can hear. They more readily accept visual input than auditory input.

Avoid confrontation if the other side takes a position with which you cannot agree. If you immediately disagree, the opposition will dig in his or her heels and become more stubborn than before. Rather, use the feel-felt-found formula: "I know how you *feel.* I once *felt* the same. But I've since *found . . .* "

Be reluctant. Pause, consider, and mull it over. Delay or table sensitive points to "think about it" or claim you need to discuss that issue with another party.

Never offer to split the difference. Let the other side make the offer. Mentioning how close you are to agreement and how patiently you have both worked usually precipitates an offer. Remember, one of your goals is to make the opposition feel good about the negotiation and the final settlement.

Develop a random concession plan. Don't set up a pattern in the way you make concessions. Avoid equal concessions. Never make big final concessions. A large concession at the very end makes it appear to the opposition as if she or he could and should have done better.

Make time your ally. Superintendents or board presidents are busy people and negotiating your contract is but one task on their agenda. Still, your contract will determine your quality of living for your tenure at the district. Nothing should be more important to you than reaching a favorable settlement. You should allow as much time as needed. Don't rush or be pushed. Take your time. The longer negotiations last, the more likely the other party will move around to your point of view. *One caution:* This works both ways. The longer the negotiations, the more likely you are to make concessions.

Check your emotions. It is a very dangerous time when you believe the negotiations are over. You are feeling good and are thus vulnerable to additional last-minute concessions. Rather than kill the deal, you might tend to agree to a point that seemed impossible earlier. To protect yourself from this situation, don't get too excited at the end of the negotiations. Keep your emotions under control.

Learn to develop walk-away power. The most powerful weapon in your negotiating arsenal is the ability to walk away. A person who sincerely believes there will be another job offer and this is not their only chance has great negotiating power. Healthy self-esteem and genuine belief in your personal worth are invaluable to successful power negotiations (Dawson, 1996).

REMEMBER, THE OFFER YOU ACCEPT WILL AFFECT YOU FOR A LIFETIME.

Hints When Negotiating the Superintendent Contract

Negotiating a superintendent's contract deserves special mention. It is unlike any other contract negotiation in the school system. You will be negotiating with the school board and most likely the school board attorney representing the board. As the incoming CEO, you will have more latitude to negotiate salary and fringe benefits than other administrators. The time will never be better to ask for large concessions than when the board is offering you your first contract. Remember and exercise the principles of power negotiations. In addition to the hints previously discussed, you should consider and follow these suggestions.

First and most important, retain a good attorney to represent you in the negotiations and the drawing up of the contract. The board will be represented by their attorney, so it is only fair that you have equal representation. Be sure that the attorney you select is versed in the school law of your state and familiar with contract language.

Second, insist on clear, specific, and well-defined provisions in your contract. Experts in school law and school contracts agree that most disagreements between superintendents and boards occurs because of contract ambiguity. A contract that reads "The superintendent will be entitled to 20 days' vacation along with school holidays" will only lead to confusion and perhaps dissention between you and the board. What does this provision mean? Does it mean that you will receive 20 vacation days over and above the designated school holidays when the schools are officially closed? Or does it mean that those 20 days include the days officially designated as school holidays? Also, just what are school holidays? Designated days or school breaks (e.g., winter break from December 23 to January 4)? Obviously, ambiguous contract language such as the example given will only lead to problems. Pay particular attention to the area of expense reimbursement. Insist that the language is specific and completely spelled out.

Third, strive to incorporate a number of special provisions in your contract. Among these are the following:

- A **multiple-year provision,** wherein your contract is in force for a number of years. Three-year contracts are most common.

- A **rollover provision,** wherein if you are not officially informed by a specific date that you are to be terminated your contract is automatically renewed.
- A **convertible insurance provision,** wherein your life and health insurance is convertible at the time of your leaving. In this case, you would be able to personally assume the premium payment(s) when you leave the district with no break in coverage. This will protect you and your family if, during your tenure with the district, a family member becomes uninsurable.
- An **irreconcilable differences or liquidation of damages clause** that specifies what compensation you will receive if you are terminated before your contract expires.

Finally, remember that you will not receive all the terms and conditions you desire in your first contract. However, you are able to add or change provisions over time. Be conscience of good timing. Negotiate changes with preferably 2 years remaining on the existing contract. Ask for more during "good times" and not during times of crisis. It is more likely that you will negotiate a raise for yourself immediately after the high school wins a coveted state championship then after a failed referendum (Cunio, Lee, & Nicholas, 1996).

Case Problem: Braving the Lion in His Den

After waiting for two days, Andra Klees finally received the phone call she had hoped would come. It was Mrs. Bea Pleasants, secretary to Superintendent Powers, calling to invite her to a meeting with Mr. Powers the following morning. No matter how much Andra pressed, Mrs. Pleasants would give no additional details. Even with limited information, Andra Klees was convinced that Superintendent Powers planned to offer her the position of Director of Special Education for his district. Andra was elated! She was sure that this was the right position for her.

But very shortly after receiving the call, Andra began to ruminate and reflect upon the seriousness of this meeting. This meeting would not only decide her immediate future, it would determine her work status and conditions for a very long time. Andra knew that Mr. Powers had a reputation of being a very strong, determined, and powerful leader who "drove a hard bargain." Mr. Powers was a lion in the position, whereas she was gentle and less experienced at negotiations.

Andra Klees wondered if they could come to a contract agreement that satisfied and pleased them both. Does Andra Klees stand a chance as she negotiates with Powers? Support your conclusions with specifics. *Write your answer below.**

*See Appendix A for one suggested response.

12

Securing the Position

Once you have acquired the position of your choice, your first priority is to secure it. Just because you get a position does not ensure that you keep it. Knowing and practicing those techniques that lock in your position are essential in the first years.

Steps to Securing Your New Position

1. Study the survey data to learn successful techniques to use to secure or lock in your new position.
2. Discuss with your mentor specific practices you could use to implement the survey techniques.
3. Use self-reflection to develop your list of successful practices.
4. Study the suggested examples to implement successful practices.
5. Combine your self-reflection list with the suggested examples to form a prioritized list of first-year activities. Make a personal commitment to do those daily.

What the Survey Data Reveal About Securing the Position

Successful administrators who acquired a desired position and then had their initial contract renewed were asked to do the following:

> List the three most important practices or techniques you used to secure your position.

Results of Their Responses
Listed in Descending Order

Successful Practices and Techniques	*Percentage*
People 1st and Tasks 2nd—schmoozing vs. working	85
Communication—being open, clear, and specific to superiors, peers, and subordinates	75
Availability to all constituents	64
Developing a positive image—remaining calm, friendly, and being one who praises	45
Asking for help and asking questions	45
Moving slowly and gently to change	40
Making the secretary your secretary	2

Conclusion

To secure your position, use the above-identified practices in the first years.

NOTE: Additional responses include acquiring a mentor, socializing with your superior, and becoming the district expert on a vital area.

Activities I Will Use to Secure My Position

After discussing with your mentor possible successful activities you should use to secure your new position, list several activities for each area identified in the survey.

Activities for **People 1st and Tasks 2nd:**

Activities for **Communication:**

Activities for **Availability:**

Activities for **Developing a Positive Image:**

Activities for **Asking for Help and Asking Questions:**

Activities for **Moving Slowly and Gently to Change:**

Activities for **Making the Secretary Your Secretary:**

Suggested Activities to Implement Successful Practices That Secure Your New Position

Suggested Activities for **People 1st and Tasks 2nd:**

- Remember that people are your business. Listening, discussing, praising, and helping is your job. You are working when you are schmoozing or "stroking" your constituents. This applies to bosses, peers, staff, parents, and students.
- Take home as much paperwork as possible. When you are "on the clock," people come first. Initially, you are judged on *who you are,* not on *what you produce.* Consider paperwork as homework and secondary to the job.

Suggested Activities for **Communications:**

- For your staff or subordinates, develop and distribute a weekly newsletter that contains upcoming events, school business, accomplishments, praise, and thanks. Send a copy to the boss.
- Schedule and regularly conduct staff meetings. Provide participants with the minutes of those meetings and any other meeting you conduct.
- Create and distribute parent and student newsletters. Use the suggestions mentioned in the first activity.
- Prepare your comments or remarks when speaking to any group. This ensures clear, organized, and professional communication.
- Use any available media—television, telephone hotline, radio, and so forth.
- Visit regularly and learn to chat. Drop by the PTA room, the lounge, the superintendent's office, and the board room.

Suggested Activities for **Availability:**

- Arrive early and leave late.
- Walk the building or premises daily.
- Inform coworkers that if your door is open they are welcome to stop by.

- Visit. See **Communication** activities above for specifics.
- Attend extracurricular and district social activities.
- Return phone calls promptly.
- Schedule parent meetings as soon as possible and allow enough time for successful conclusion.

Suggested Activities for **Developing a Positive Image:**

- Remain calm in times of crisis. Act decisively and speak slowly, clearly, and in short sentences. Never yell—even when angry or frustrated. Yelling only labels you as irrational or not in control of yourself.
- Never betray a confidence. What an individual confides to you stays with you. This practice applies to parents/students, staff, fellow administrators, and your superiors.
- Smile and laugh. Although there are times to be serious, there are also times to enjoy and to share positive feelings.
- Say what you mean and do what you say. Studies indicate that this one practice does more to build trust than any other practice.
- Look and dress like the administrator you are. You have a role that may be enhanced or tarnished by your appearance. Slim, well-groomed, and properly dressed administrators command more respect and have a more positive image than overweight, ill-clothed, sloppy administrators.

Suggested Activities for **Asking for Help and Asking Questions:**

- Develop a democratic administrative style. Foster shared decision making with your staff. Let experts assume leadership roles.
- Don't be ashamed to ask questions when you don't know. No one knows everything, and being new to a position implies that there are many practices and behaviors of which you are unaware. Ask people in the know. Usually, people are flattered when you solicit their knowledge.
- Asking for needed help from all constituents only builds morale and camaraderie. Being able to help a colleague or a boss acts as an ego booster for all. Actively seek and encourage helping situations.

Suggested Activities for **Moving Slowly and Gently to Change:**

- Remember that most people fear change, and they may be fearful that you, as a new administrator, will make unnecessary and indiscriminate changes. If at all possible, wait to implement change until you have established your own credibility and leadership position.
- Institute needed change as a "we" change, not as an "I" change. Use consensus to implement change. If change is required or imposed from above (new law, school board policy, etc.), honestly share that information with your staff and then implement together.

Suggested Activities for **Making the Secretary Your Secretary:**

- If at all possible, choose your own secretary.
- If you inherit the secretary from your predecessor, meet with the secretary and spell out your views of the position.
- Regardless of how you acquire your secretary, within the first few days on the job, review the job description and prioritize those duties you believe are essential to the position. If you feel that office confidentiality and mutual loyalty are essential, tell the secretary. If you give top priority to serving people rather than to clerical/word-processing tasks, explain that to your secretary. Be specific. Spell out preferable visitor and telephone etiquette. That might include requesting that the secretary stop typing when a visitor arrives and offer assistance.
- Provide time and money for your secretary's professional development. Encourage and provide the resources for your secretary to attend skill workshops and training sessions.
- Reward positive performance. Raises and bonuses are always welcomed. But even if you cannot award raises and bonuses for excellent performance, you can praise, give small gifts of appreciation, and provide compensation time. Do it!

My Final List of Activities to Secure My New Position

Combine your list of activities and the suggested activities provided. Write your final list of activities you are committed to practice to secure your new position in the first few years.

Activities for **People 1st and Tasks 2nd:**

Activities for **Communication:**

Activities for **Availability:**

Activities for **Developing a Positive Image:**

Activities for **Asking for Help and Asking Questions:**

Activities for **Moving Slowly and Gently to Change:**

Activities for **Making the Secretary Your Secretary:**

Case Problem: Ben Scrood

Ben Scrood still couldn't believe his misfortune! How could this happen to him? Yesterday, his immediate supervisor, Assistant Superintendent Michael Hatchetman, curtly informed him that the school board would not be renewing his contract for the next school year. When Ben asked for an explanation, Hatchetman would only say that there had been a number of complaints about his effectiveness and fairness as a principal. He added that the dissatisfaction was widespread and included teachers, noncertified staff, and some parents. Hatchetman further admitted that it was his duty to report all complaints and problems to the school board. When Ben demanded specifics, he was told that giving him such information would be a breech of confidentiality and therefore impossible. Hatchetman concluded the discussion by stating that it just wasn't a good match between Ben and the district.

This morning, Ben Scrood tried to understand what could have gone that wrong to cause his being fired. He wrote down a list of honest positives and negatives during his one-year tenure as principal. Under "Positives," he listed the following:

- Successfully implemented four major changes requested by the superintendent and Hatchetman during this first year
- Believed that 37 out of 40 teachers approved of him. Most seemed to like him, and most were cooperative.
- Completed all managerial tasks correctly and in a timely fashion
- Wrote and was awarded five grants totaling over $85,000
- Did all his own word processing and bookkeeping because the secretary couldn't use the computer, made serious mistakes, and was the sister of a long-standing board member
- Made more repairs and got more materials and supplies for the staff than any principal in the district
- Provided numerous staff development opportunities for the faculty and even had a holiday party for the staff at his home.
- Etc., etc., etc.!!!

Under "Negatives," he listed the following:

- Three teachers opposed any action he took. They didn't want to change. They didn't like him. They were vocal and well-known teachers in the district.
- His secretary was incompetent and disloyal, but Hatchetman advised him to keep her on because she was very well connected.
- He knew he was not Hatchetman's first choice for the position. Hatchetman had given him a predictive administrator effectiveness test, and he had performed marginally. Hatchetman had backed the candidate who scored best on the assessment instrument but was overruled by the superintendent who listened to community supporters. Would Hatchetman be so petty and unprofessional as to hold this against Ben?

After reading his list several times, Ben Scrood was frustrated and perplexed. He knew the pluses far outweighed the minuses. He couldn't see where any one of the negatives warranted dismissal. He had no clue. Did he deserve to be fired, or was Ben . . . ? Analyze the available information to determine what happened to Ben. Why do you think he was fired? Could he have prevented this tragedy? *Write your answer below.**

*See Appendix A for one suggested response.

APPENDIX A

Suggested Responses to Case Problems

Chapter 1: What I Need

These are the tasks I would want my mentor to do to help me secure the right position in school administration:

- Be there. Be available. Return my calls and meet when necessary.
- Openly share knowledge and expertise. Pull no punches when talking together.
- Encourage. Believe in me and my potential. Praise good performance.
- Demand high standards. Insist that I do my best.
- Critique any crucial correspondence.
- Provide insider information about local districts.
- Make a call when appropriate and when it might do me some good.
- Commiserate for a while when things go wrong but then direct me to the next goal.
- Be willing to role-play a mock interview and negotiation meeting.
- Honestly and candidly critique a video of my mock interview presentation.
- Be caring, patient, and generous!

Chapter 2: Will B. Mobile

Suggested areas in order of presentation for a professional résumé are these:

- Personal information: name, address, phone, fax, e-mail, and so forth
- Goal (optional)
- Education

- Valid certifications and licenses held
- Administrative experience (listed in reverse chronological order, starting with the most recent), with highlights of duties and special accomplishments
- Other related work experience (i.e., teaching experience)
- Other positions of leadership
- Awards, organizations, personal activities (optional)
- References listing three or four individuals' positions and phone numbers (plus a statement that others are available on request)

Chapter 3: Michelle La Creme

To successfully secure and retain a leadership position of principal, an individual must have self-confidence and high self-esteem. One way to boost Michelle's opinion of herself is to have her review her remarkable accomplishments either alone or with you. This exercise should put her perceived lack of experience into proportion with her other characteristics. Hopefully, Michelle La Creme will come to this conclusion on her own. However, if she still doesn't believe her qualifications are superb, it is up to you to point out the obvious to her. Michelle must be made to understand that **she is La Creme De La Creme.**

Chapter 4: Van Ity

Claiming that you have only strengths and refusing to acknowledge weaknesses could send a negative message to listeners. Interviewers could wonder what Van Ity has to hide, or they might conclude that he is so egotistical or vain that he is incapable of being truthful or admitting his humanism. Don't let vanity get in the way of success. Admit that you are human and have more to learn.

One way to express your limitations is to address them as follows:

- Areas you are presently working to improve
- Weaknesses in professional skills rather than personal faults

An example of this approach is "I find that the technology in computer graphics has grown so rapidly in the past 6 months that I'm beginning to fall behind. To stop the bleeding, I've just enrolled in a class at State College to keep me up to date."

Chapter 5: Roll With the Punches

It is impossible to control all the factors when job hunting. It is also naive to expect that every situation will favor your candidacy, even if you are well prepared. There is nothing Shirley Bend can do to change the room arrangement or the composition of the selection committee, but she can use two axioms when coping with this difficult and potentially unfavorable hurdle.

First, she must disregard the negatives and concentrate on the positive aspects of this situation. Positive thinking works and should not be dismissed as an old wives' tale. Examples of possible positives are that a teacher and a woman are present, Firman was friendly and professional, the principal's name is Smiles, and Shirley does excel at speaking in small groups.

Finally, Shirley Bend must practice what her name implies. She needs to be bendable, flexible, agile, and lithe. Shirley Bend must roll with the punches.

Chapter 6: Think Before You Speak

Remembering that men and women communicate (give and receive information) differently, apply what you learned in this section and think before you speak. Take a deep breath or swallow before you blurt. Under pressure, it is difficult to organize your thoughts before you speak, and many people tend to plunge in. But, thought organizing is a skill you must learn, if not master, to interview successfully. Consider employing *opening sentences or phrases* to allow yourself time to organize an answer or response. Some opening sentences are "That's an excellent question. Give me a minute to organize my thoughts" and "I'm not sure what you are asking. Would you elaborate?"

Chapter 7: Arndt Sure

Sexual harassment means all unwanted sexual behavior. It includes any conduct not solicited or encouraged by the worker—in this case, Arndt Sure—that is offensive or undesirable. Sexual harassment may be perpetrated by any coworker, including a peer—in this case, Ginger DeVamp. It may occur on or off the job site. Because Arndt finds Ginger's behavior sexually unwanted, undesirable, and offensive, this is a case of sexual harassment.

Arndt should inform Ginger that her behavior is unwanted, that he finds her behavior offensive, and that he believes it is a form of sexual harassment. If she does not immediately desist, he should follow the steps outlined in *Appropriate Actions When You Are the Victim of Harassment* in this section.

Note: *One caution.* Although this is the best course of action, be aware that any time you accuse another of sexual harassment, it could backfire and the person in turn might try to accuse you.

Chapter 8: Start With a Plan

M. T. Head has a dual search challenge. First, he must find suitable areas to settle and then must learn about and apply for the open administrative positions. These tasks are not that difficult with the information sources available today. Because M. T. wishes to stay within the state, it limits his choices and becomes a rural statewide search.

Most state departments of education have readily available demographic profiles available for each county, township, and city/town. They constantly gather information regarding their schools, constituents, growth patterns, and so on. This information is available on request at little or no cost in hard copy as well as through computer service lines. Statistical information and current maps may also be procured from various state agencies. State departments of education along with state universities provide written or on-line school administrative job openings on a regular basis. Many school districts have their own web site, which is accessible for examination.

Without leaving his office, M. T. Head may gather a great deal of initial information in the two areas that pertain to his needs. After pinpointing potential relocation sites, he may wish to take short day or weekend trips to scout out these areas more thoroughly. He could combine them with short vacation holidays that he shares with his daughter. M. T. would then have an initial plan with which to start.

Chapter 9: Barry Tight

Barry Tight has his priorities backward. He knows he should dress appropriately for the forthcoming interview, but he refuses to make this a priority. This behavior fits the old saying "Penny wise but pound foolish." If his old suit cannot be properly altered, it is time to invest in one new suit. He should view it as a necessary investment in the future and not a luxury. Besides, he will find many good uses for the suit as the new middle school principal. **Now is not the time to be tight, Barry!**

Review of appropriate appearance when interviewing:

- Men
  - Attire:
    - Dark suit
    - White or off-white shirt
    - Conservative tie
    - Minimal jewelry—watch and wedding ring, if applicable
    - Matching socks
    - Black or dark brown leather dress shoes
  - Grooming:
    - Freshly cut and washed hair
    - Clean shaven or neatly trimmed facial hair
    - Clean and trimmed nails
- Women
  - Attire:
    - Dark blue suit
    - White or off-white blouse
    - Dark blue mid-high heels
    - Neutral-toned stockings
    - Minimal jewelry—watch, wedding ring, if applicable, and small or no earrings

Grooming:
Clean and styled "daytime" hair
Daytime makeup
Conservative (clear or muted) polished nails cut to sport length

For more specific suggestions on acceptable attire and grooming tips, see Molloy's (1988) book *New Dress for Success,* listed in the Bibliography.

Chapter 10: Smelling Like a Rose

Although with reflection and advance preparation you can predict more than 80% of the questions asked at the interview, there will always be some questions you did not predict and a few that seem unrelated or strange. Some districts admit that they throw in an unusual question in hopes of seeing how candidates react under pressure. So be it.

Dr. Rose Thomas-Brown can use a number of speaking techniques to deal with this situation and come out smelling like a rose. Here are some suggested tips:

- Don't waste your time feeling shocked, betrayed, or treated poorly. Get on with the job of answering. Practice prior to the interview should include a few "off the wall" questions so that you can practice fielding them.
- If confronted with a question for which you have no immediate response, use an *introductory sentence* to give yourself time to gather your thoughts. Rose might begin by saying, "That's a very interesting and surprising question. Let me take a minute to think."
- Two other techniques you may use to gain time is a *clarifying question* and *reiteration.* Rose might reply, "I'm not sure I understand. Do you want me to tell you about my outside readings?"
- Don't rush. Take your time and focus. Deliver the best answer you can give at the time. All who have ever interviewed will probably admit that given a second chance they would have answered a question differently and better. That's normal. Just do your best and move on.

Chapter 11: Braving the Lion in His Den

Of course, Andra Klees will negotiate a favorable contract with Mr. Powers. She has read and digested this section and now has the tools and information necessary to be successful. Much like Androcles in Aesop's fable, *Androcles and the Lion,* Andra Klees might be a mouse compared to the lion, Mr. Powers, but she has knowledge, skill, persistence, and a positive attitude.

Chapter 12: Ben Scrood

This case is an abbreviated retelling of a true story in which the names were changed to protect the individuals. That Ben Scrood ever had a real chance to be successful is doubtful. However, there are a number of practices he could have used to increase his chances. Obviously, hindsight and distance makes this task much simpler for us than it was for Ben, who lived this misadventure.

Although Ben could only identify and list three negatives, they were very powerful and destructive. Any one of them could sink an administrator's chance for success. Having a secretary who is "connected," incompetent, disloyal, and untrustworthy makes the job impossible. Insisting at the time of hiring that you be allowed to choose your own secretary is a wise policy and the best one to avoid this disaster. Being a novice administrator, Ben did not understand how important a good secretary is to every administrator. After being stuck with her and having no freedom to maneuver, Ben should have fired her or preferably insisted that the district transfer her at once. This might seem like a foolhardy move, but there appears to be no other choice. He would have to take his chances when it came to backlash from the school board and staff. This is a situation that cannot be ignored or endured.

The problem of having a few vocal, powerful, dissatisfied teachers is common for all principals. Ben could have done a number of things differently to defuse this situation. First, he should have moved much more slowly to implement change, thereby giving the detractors less about which to complain. He could have spent much more time schmoozing his entire staff. This would have solidified his lock with the majority and might have turned around his detractors.

Finally, the apparent bias on the part of Ben's immediate supervisor, Mr. Hatchetman, is an interpersonal skills task for Ben. It is conceivable that Hatchetman would never give Ben a fair chance, but there are a number of things that might have reversed the situation. Some positive actions that Ben might have attempted include seeking Hatchetman's advice and help, asking questions, taking time to be social with him, and dropping by regularly to report in and just visit. Also, Ben needed to do the same with the superintendent and the school board members. It would be very difficult for Hatchetman to malign Ben if his bosses were Ben's supporters.

APPENDIX B

Information Sources for Sexual Harassment Issues

American Association of University Women
Education on Sexual Harassment
2401 Virginia Avenue, NW
Washington, DC 20037
(202) 785-7700

American Bar Association
Commission on Women
750 North Lake Shore Drive
Chicago, IL 60611
(312) 988-5668

American Civil Liberties Union
Women's Rights Project
132 West 43rd Street
New York, NY 10036
(212) 944-9800

Center for Women and Policy Studies
2000 P Street, NW, Suite 508
Washington, DC 20036
(202) 293-1100

Equal Employment Opportunity Commission (EEOC)*
National Headquarters
Washington Field Office
1400 L Street NW, Suite 200
Washington, DC 20005
(202) 275-7377

*The EEOC has a field office in most major cities across America. Call information for the closest major city to you.

Equal Rights Advocates
1663 Mission Street, Suite 550
San Francisco, CA 94103
(415) 621-0505

Lawyers' Committee for Civil Rights Under the Law
1400 I Street, NW, Suite 400
Washington, DC, 20005
(202) 321-1212

NAACP Legal Defense and Education Fund, Inc.
99 Hudson Street
New York, NY 10013
(212) 219-1900

NOW Legal Defense Fund
National Association of Women and the Law
99 Hudson Street, 12th Floor
New York, NY 10013
(212) 925-6636

Bibliography

American Psychiatric Association. (1994). *Diagnostic and statistical manual–IV.* Washington, DC: Author.

Ashby, D., Kosmoski, G. J., Love, R., & Esperanza, Z. (Speakers). (1998). *How to interview successfully if you're not a white male* (Cassette Recording No. AASA 98-61). San Diego: American Association of School Administrators.

Austin, N. K. (1996, March). The new job interview: Beyond the trick question. *Working Woman,* pp. 23-24.

Baxter, R. (1985). *Sexual harassment in the workplace: A guide to law, revised.* New York: Executive Enterprises Publications.

Cann, A., Siegfried, W., & Pearce, L. (1981). Forced attention to specific applicant qualifications: Impact on physical attractiveness and sex of applicant biases. *Personnel Psychology, 34*(1), 65-75.

Cunio, T., Lee, R., & Nicholas, E. (Speakers). (1996). *Negotiating your contract—Get it done right* (Cassette Recording No. AASA 96–161). San Diego: American Association of School Administrators.

Dawson, R. (1996, March). Secrets of power negotiating. *Working Woman,* Special Book Section.

Equal Employment Opportunity Commission. (1990). *Guidelines in sexual harassment.* Washington, DC: Author.

Eskenazi, M., & Gallen, D. (1991). *Sexual harassment: Know your rights.* New York: Carroll & Graf.

Glickman, C. D. (1990). Preface. In T. M. Bey & C. Thomas Holmes (Eds.), *Mentoring: Developing successful teachers.* Reston, VA: Association of Teacher Educators.

Goodlad, J. (1990). *Teachers for our nation's schools.* San Francisco: Jossey-Bass.

Haefner, J. (1977). Race, age, sex, and competence as factors in employer selection of the disadvantaged. *Journal of Applied Psychology, 62*(2), 199-202.

Hall, G. (1992). Induction: The missing link. *Journal of Education, 33*(3), 53-55.

Healy, C., & Welchert, A. (1990). Mentoring relations: A definition to advance research and practice. *Educational Researcher, 19*(9), 17-21.

Heiberger, M. M., & Vick, J. M. (1992). *The academic job search handbook.* Philadelphia: University of Pennsylvania Press.

Hill, A. (1991). The nature of the beast. In M. Eskenazi & D. Gallen, *Sexual harassment: Know your rights.* New York: Carroll & Graf.

Huling-Austin, L. (1990). Mentoring is squishy business. In T. Bey & C. Thomas Holmes (Eds.), *Mentoring: Developing successful teachers.* Reston, VA: Association of Teacher Educators.

Kosmoski, G. J. (1997). *Supervision.* Mequon, WI: Stylex.

Kosmoski, G. J., Estep, S., & Pollack, D. (Speakers). (1997). *How to land the right position in school administration* (Cassette Recording No. NASSP 97-253). Orlando, FL: National Association of Secondary School Principals.

Kosmoski, G. J., & Pollack, D. R. (Speakers). (1996). *How women school administrators can interview successfully* (Cassette Recording No. AASA 96-402). San Diego: American Association of School Administrators.

Kosmoski, G. J., & Pollack, D. R. (1997). *Effects of a mentoring program for beginning school administrators.* Hilton Head, SC: Eastern Educational Research Association.

Kosmoski, G. J., & Pollack, D. R. (1998, March). *Developing leaders: Positive effects of a mentoring program for beginning school administrators.* Paper presented at the annual meeting of the Association for Supervision and Curriculum Development, San Antonio, Texas.

Kremer, T. G. (1996, March). *Preparing for the interview—Where to get good information.* Paper presented at the annual meeting of the American Association of School Administrators, San Diego.

Lakoff, R. T. (1990). *Talking power: The politics of language in our lives.* New York: Basic Books.

Lifetime Television Network. (1996, May). *Final take: Sexual harassment* [Documentary]. New York: Lifetime Television.

MacKinnon, C. (1992). Sexual harassment: The experience. In M. Eskenazi & D. Gallen, *Sexual harassment: Know your rights.* New York: Carroll & Graf.

Mann, J. (1994). *The difference: Growing up female in America.* New York: Warner Books.

Merriam, S. (1993). Mentor and proteges. A critical review of the literature. *Adult Education Quarterly, 33*(3), 161-173.

Molloy, J. T. (1988). *New dress for success.* New York: Warner Books.

Nelson, M. B. (1994). *The stronger women get, the more men love football: Sexism and the American culture of sports.* New York: Harcourt Brace.

Nierenberg, G. I. (1981). *The art of negotiating.* New York: Simon & Schuster.

Résumés, applications, forms, cover letters, and interviews. (1993). Washington, DC: Government Printing Office.

Tannen, D. (1994). *Talking 9 to 5. Women and men in the workplace: Language, sex and power.* New York: Avon Books.

Williams, C. (1992). The glass escalator: Hidden advantages for men. *Social Problems, 39*(3), 253-267.

Zebrowitz, L., Tenenbaum, D., & Goldstein, L. (1991). The impact of job applicants' facial maturity, gender, and academic achievement on hiring recommendations. *Journal of Applied Social Psychology, 21*(7), 525-548.

The Corwin Press logo—a raven striding across an open book—represents the happy union of courage and learning. We are a professional-level publisher of books and journals for K–12 educators, and we are committed to creating and providing resources that embody these qualities. Corwin's motto is "Success for All Learners."